HEIST

AN INSIDE LOOK AT THE WORLD'S 100 GREATEST HEISTS, CONS, AND CAPERS

FROM BURGLARIES TO BANK JOBS AND EVERYTHING IN BETWEEN

WHALEN
BOOK·WORKS

BY PETE STEGEMEYER | **ILLUSTRATIONS BY REBECCA PRY**

Whalen Book Works
68 North Street
Kennebunkport, ME 04046

www.whalenbookworks.com

Cover design by Steve Cooley and Bryce de Flamand
Interior design by Bryce de Flamand
Illustrations by Rebecca Pry
Photography: Page 4 & 86, photo by Andrew Neel on Unsplash; page 8, photo by Thaynara Souza on Unsplash; pages 56 & 192, photos used under official license from iStock.com; pages 120 & 172 photos used under official license from Shutterstock.com; page 171, photo by Viktor Forgacs on Unsplash
Typography: Baskerville URW, Impact, Futura PT, and Trade Gothic LT Std

Printed in the United States of America

1 2 3 4 5 6 7 8 9 0

First Edition

TO CHRISTINA, WHOM I PROMISED I
WOULDN'T MAKE ANY CHEESY JOKES
ABOUT STEALING MY HEART.

CONTENTS

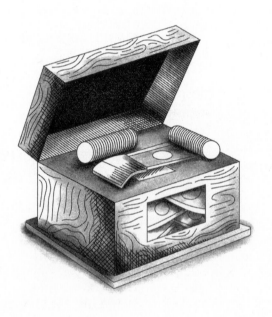

INTRODUCTION

When I was a freshman in high school, I got caught looking at one of my friend's *Playboys*. Even more embarrassingly, I was caught reading one of the articles (people really do that!). That article was my first introduction to the Stopwatch Gang, a team of daring bank robbers who, as the name implies, used a stopwatch to ensure they never spent more time in the bank than they needed to avoid capture. I was amazed that people could interview bank robbers and get them to tell their stories, and I couldn't believe that people got to write stories that made crime seem so cool, but from the first time I read that article, I was hooked. I never imagined that one day I'd be doing the same thing, but here we are.

For as long as I can remember, there has always been something fascinating to me about heists. The idea that someone could sneak into a building and bypass seemingly impossible security systems completely undetected just felt like magic, or the closest thing the real world has to someone like James Bond. Many of the heists in this book do feel like something out of a flashy movie, while others more closely resemble *Dumb and Dumber*, but each of them is fascinating in their own way. For me, a heist is about more than what is being taken, it's about how it's done. If I can say it in the corniest way possible, it's about the journey more than the destination.

While I may be waxing poetic about heists and burglars, I feel that it's important to mention that the intent of this book is not to romanticize theft, but instead to share some of the stories that have long fascinated me, and I hope will fascinate you as well. I have tried to compile a collection of heists, cons, and scams from around the world that I hope serve as cautionary tales—both to dissuade you from pulling off a heist of your own and to help you identify the hallmarks of popular scams so you don't fall victim to them yourself.

Writing this book has been a dream come true, and I hope you enjoy reading it as much as I have loved writing it.

—*Pete Stegemeyer*

CHAPTER 1

PLANES, TRAINS, AND AUTOMOBILES

Not every heist takes place in a bank or museum. In fact, some of history's most iconic heists involve targets on the move. From the world's first train robbery to D. B. Cooper's infamous airplane hijacking, this chapter is all about capers where the journey is as important as the destination. Whether you're coming by land, air, or sea, these heists are too good to pass up.

THE GREAT GOLD TRAIN ROBBERY OF 1855

A classic example of the ol' switcheroo.

1855 ★ *UNITED KINGDOM*

DESCRIPTION

The South Eastern Railway (SER) was formed in 1836 to provide train service between London and Folkestone, near Dover. Construction of the route began in 1838, and several stretches of the track were built simultaneously. The railroad grew quickly, often acquiring or absorbing other rail companies, and becoming a popular line for boat trains and for people trying to find a safe and reliable way to transport their goods from London to Paris.

Each day, at least four trains ran the line from London to Folkestone, terminating at the docks where steamboats would carry passengers and cargo across the English Channel and then on to a train that led to Paris.

The railway's reputation so prestigious that when the owners learned that one of their employees was a gambler, he was fired immediately. However, no level of caution could protect the railway's most precious cargo from a team of determined thieves, and in May 1855, two hundred pounds of gold left London, but two hundred pounds of steel and lead entered Paris.

KNOWN SUSPECTS

William Pierce worked at the London Bridge Station and had a history of involvement in low-level crimes and generally shady behavior, as well as a penchant for "loud waistcoats and fancy trousers," according to historian Donald Thomas. After being fired, Pierce started working as a ticket printer at a betting office, but he continued to frequent the same bars he always had. He heard about shipments of gold being sent to Paris via the railway, and before long he began putting together a plan.

Pierce knew stealing the gold wouldn't be an easy task. Beyond being under constant supervision by guards, it was packed into wooden boxes that were bound with iron bands and then covered with a wax seal that displayed the coat of arms of the gold merchants. These bouillon boxes were weighed at several points along the journey and were locked inside of a set of three specially designed safes that featured 2.5-inch-thick steel walls and could only be opened with two complex keys. Copies of these keys were kept at the London Bridge and Folkestone offices, and company policy prevented anyone from having both keys at the same time.

Pierce realized that if stealing the gold were going to be possible, he'd need to bring in someone else. He found a partner in a man named Edward Agar. Agar was a burglar and safecracker who had been working as a professional thief for over twenty years.

At first, Agar shot down the plan as being too far-fetched. He then left on a trip to the United States and Australia. After he returned a few years later, Pierce brought the idea

up again. This time, Agar admitted it might be possible, but only if they could get the keys copied and if they could get both a guard and a general manager from SER on board with the plan.

Pierce continued to spend more time at the train bar, and eventually overheard James Burgess, a guard that often worked on the gold shipments. Burgess was a respected man, happily married and aboveboard. He had a reputation for being thrifty, but thrifty men still need to feed their families, and when the gold boom died down, the railway cut his wages. When Agar and Pierce offered him a cut of the gold, Burgess quickly agreed.

Next, they found a man named William Tester, who worked in the traffic department as the assistant to the superintendent at the London Bridge Station. Tester was well-educated and sought to improve his station in life. He was what was known at the time as a dandy, a middle-class person who yearned for the finer things. He often wore a monocle and tried to present himself as upper class, so when the team approached him with an opportunity to become legitimately wealthy, he couldn't resist.

In May 1854, Pierce and Agar traveled to Folkestone to observe how the gold was loaded onto the trains. Unfortunately for them, they were detected almost immediately for looking suspicious, and both the municipal and railway police were alerted. Pierce returned to London, and Agar remained in Folkestone to continue his research alone. Before long, he determined that one of the keys was carried by the Folkestone superintendent, and the other was locked in a cabinet at the Folkestone station offices on the piers.

In July 1854 a steamboat captain lost his keys, forcing the railway to get the safes sent back to the Chubb Company to get new locks and keys made. It just so happened that the man tasked with this job was William Tester. Tester made impressions of the keys in wax, and then sent them off to the end stations. Unfortunately, Tester made duplicates of the same key twice, so the men still needed to get their hands on the second key.

Agar, not wanting to leave anything else to chance, purchased £200 in gold with his own money and arranged to have it shipped along the route while using one of his aliases, E. E. Archer. Under this name, Agar traveled with the gold to Folkestone and then went to the office to collect it. Once in the office, he watched the manager open a cupboard to get the safe key. Agar came back a few days later to open the cupboard and make a wax impression of the second key.

Once they had impressions of both keys, Agar and Pierce created rough copies, and then used files to refine them until they worked

perfectly. Burgess tested the keys in the locks while riding the routes he worked until they were finally satisfied with every set of keys.

By the spring of 1855, the team was ready; they just needed to wait until there was a large shipment to steal. Tester, who was in charge of the schedules, assigned Burgess to work every night shift in May. Burgess would see how much gold was loaded each night, and if there was a sufficient haul, Burgess would send a signal out by stepping onto the train platform and wiping his face with a white handkerchief.

On the night of May 15, 1855, Burgess gave the signal. Agar and Pierce purchased first-class tickets, giving their bags to Burgess to store with him in the guard's car. As the train departed, Pierce took his seat and Agar hid in the guard car under a pile of clothes. Once the train was moving, Agar sprang into action, knowing he only had thirty-five minutes to work until the next station. Agar pulled out his keys to open the safe and discovered that only one of the locks actually was locked; this was apparently a common practice, due to the annoying security features.

Agar used pliers to rip out the rivets holding the iron bands on the boxes, and used wedges to open the lid without causing visible damage. He then emptied out the gold, weighed it with scales he'd brought with him, and replaced the exact weight of stolen gold with lead buckshot. He then renailed the iron bands, resealed the wax seal, and packed the bullion boxes back into the safe.

Once Agar was done, he hid back under a pile of clothes as the train pulled into Redhill Station, where more gold was loaded onto the train. The first bag of stolen gold was given to Tester, who took it with him to the London offices, so he could be seen and have an alibi. Pierce moved from the first-class cabin to the guard car to join the team. The train left Redhill, and Agar and Pierce went to work on the second two boxes of gold. These boxes actually contained so much gold that Agar had to leave some in the last box because they didn't have enough lead to make up the weight. Once they were done, the three men cleaned up the crime scene to remove traces of wood splinters and wax. They strapped the bags of gold to their bodies and then covered up with cloaks and moved back to the first-class cabin. In total, they'd stolen around 224 pounds of gold, valued at the time at around £12,000. That much gold today would be worth about $6 million dollars.

The men departed the train at Folkestone, and the bullion boxes continued onto Paris, where they were weighed. One box came in at forty pounds underweight, and the other two came in a bit heavier than they originally were. The boxes were opened, the lead shot was discovered, and word got back to London quickly. However, the men were so thorough, that the police couldn't determine who had pulled off the crime. It even took them months to discover that the crime had happened on the British side of the journey.

Meanwhile, Pierce and Agar sold some of the gold, mostly the American Eagle coins, but were smart enough to not sell all of it right away, or to try to unload any of the larger bars. Instead of selling these bars, they decided to build a smelter in the home that Agar shared with his girlfriend, a prostitute named Fanny Kay. Unfortunately, the smelter cracked and molten gold started leaking onto the floor, starting a fire. This was too much for Fanny, and she left Agar. He moved in with Pierce and they continued selling the

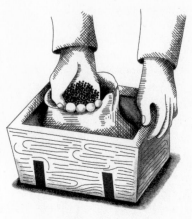

gold, but this time, they used a fence, who broke things up evenly between the four men. Burgess and Tester used this money to buy bonds and stocks, while Pierce used his money to open a betting shop.

Soon after the robbery, Tester took a new job working for the Swedish Railway, and Burgess was questioned, but quickly ruled out because of his fourteen years of service to the company.

Agar fell in love with a new prostitute; this time it was nineteen-year-old Emily Campbell. Emily's pimp was none too pleased with this, but Agar offered to loan him money to smooth things over. However, when Agar came to collect, the pimp, a man named William Humphreys, set him up, and Agar was arrested and charged with check forgery because the police didn't know how else he'd have so much money. Agar was found guilty and sentenced to life in the Australian penal colony.

As Agar was awaiting his deportation, he arranged with his lawyer to provide Pierce with the £3,000 in his bank account, so that Pierce could give it to Fanny to help support her and their child. Pierce agreed, and made a few payments to Fanny, but soon just kept the money for himself. This angered Fanny, and she went

to the police and told them that she knew who had pulled off the heist. When police didn't believe her, she took them to her home and showed them the floor that still had burn marks and gold that had solidified into the wood.

Agar was questioned about his involvement in the crime, but he refused to cooperate. However, once he learned that Pierce had failed to keep his word and pay Fanny, he actually turned Queen's evidence and provided the full details of the crime. In November 1856, Pierce and Burgess were arrested. Tester, who was living in Sweden, couldn't be extradited, but when he heard police wanted to speak to him, he was fired from his new railway job and returned to London, where he was quickly arrested.

Pierce, Burgess, and Tester pleaded not guilty, and during their trials Agar testified against each of them and tried to repent to the court for being what historian Donald Thomas described as a "self-confessed professional criminal who had not made an honest living since the age of 18." Other witnesses, including several of the bar patrons and railway workers, said that they often saw these men together, and the jury deliberated for less than ten minutes. Each was found guilty. Pierce was convicted of larceny and burgess, and Tester was convicted of larceny as a servant. During the sentencing, the judge, Sir Samuel Martin, actually released a statement about Agar and his talents as a thief, saying, "The man Agar is a man who is as bad, I dare say, as bad can be, but that he is a man of most extraordinary ability no person who heard him examined can for a moment deny . . . "

THE CASE TODAY

Pierce was sentenced to two years of hard labor in England, with three months in solitary confinement. Burgess and Tester were both sentenced to fourteen years in Australia, but both were given tickets of leave and pardons after less than two years. Agar was not charged with the crime, but the court decided to still uphold the now demonstrably bunk check fraud conviction, and he was sent back to Australia. He received leave in 1860 and moved to Ceylon (now Sri Lanka).

THE FIRST SWEDISH SPEEDBOAT HEIST

Thieves made a big splash during this heist.

DECEMBER 22, 2000 ★ *SWEDEN*

DESCRIPTION

On December 22, 2000, just before 5:00 p.m., a car bomb exploded in front of the Grand Hotel in Stockholm. Within seconds, a second car bomb rocked the nearby Stand Hotel. Police scrambled to the sites of the explosions.

Minutes later, on the other side of town, a man walked into the National Museum and pulled out an MP5, a small submachine gun (you might recognize the model from the movie *Die Hard*). He used the gun to threaten the security guards into submission while two other men, who had been posing as museum guests, grabbed three paintings off the wall, brandishing their own handguns.

With the paintings in hand, all three men ran out of the front door, scattered nails in the street in front of the museum to slow down police cars, and then ran across the street

to a speedboat that they'd moored in the river. They made their escape, without firing a shot or hurting a single person. The entire heist lasted barely a few minutes. The boat would eventually be found by police after the thieves abandoned it, but by then they were long gone.

The thieves made off with three paintings: *Conversation with the Gardener* and *Young Parisian* by Renoir and a self-portrait by Rembrandt. Altogether, the haul was worth $30 to $40 million dollars.

A few days after the heist, the thieves issued a ransom demand to the museum for $3 million. This might seem low considering the value of the works, but it's actually a pretty good price for a ransom, because trying to sell these paintings on the black market would be incredibly difficult due to the paintings' notoriety. Even

if a sale were arranged, the thieves would not get anywhere near what the paintings were worth.

The museum refused to pay the ransom, and the two men who submitted the ransom request—a pair of lawyers that had been hired to act as middlemen for the thieves—were arrested shortly after.

KNOWN SUSPECTS

Within a month of the heist, ten arrests had been made, including a Russian man in his early forties named Alex Petrov. He was the supposed ringleader of the gang and was the man who entered the museum with the MP5. Petrov was sentenced to six-and-a-half years in prison. Another gunman, Stefan Nordstroem, received six years for his part in the crime. A few months later, in 2001, the first painting, Renoir's *Conversation*, was found hidden in a duffel bag during a drug raid. The other paintings would only be found years later.

THE CASE TODAY

In 2005, four men—two Iraqis, a Swede, and a Gambian—were arrested in Copenhagen trying to sell the Rembrandt self-portrait to undercover police. Following the sting, the FBI announced the recovery of the remaining Renoir earlier that year in Los Angeles. All three paintings were recovered in good condition, an exceptionally happy outcome for art heists.

In total, thirteen men were charged in connection to the heist, and several of them were sentenced relatively harshly by Swedish standards, since this heist was the first known armed robbery of the kind in the country's history.

★ ★ ★

WHERE WE'RE GOING WE DON'T NEED ROADS

WHAT: SPEEDBOATS ★ WHEN: 1890–TODAY ★ WHERE: STOCKHOLM, SWEDEN

IT MIGHT SEEM CRAZY FOR STOCKHOLM TO HAVE SUCH A RICH HISTORY OF BOAT-RELATED HEISTS, BUT GEOGRAPHICALLY SPEAKING, A GETAWAY BOAT IS PROBABLY YOUR BEST BET IN STOCKHOLM—UNLESS YOU CAN GET A HELICOPTER. THE CITY OF STOCKHOLM ACTUALLY SITS ON THE DELTA WHERE LAKE MALAREN MEETS THE BALTIC SEA AND CONSISTS OF A SERIES OF FOURTEEN ISLANDS. AS A RESULT, MUCH OF THE CITY IS FILLED WITH CANALS AND RIVERS WITH EASY SEA ACCESS, AND UNLIKE VENICE, MOST ARE WIDE ENOUGH TO TRAVERSE EASILY. THE GREATER LAKE MALAREN DELTA ACTUALLY CONTAINS OVER 1,200 INDIVIDUAL ISLANDS AND SPANS OVER 440 SQUARE MILES BEFORE REACHING THE BALTIC SEA, MAKING IT INCREDIBLY DIFFICULT TO FIND PEOPLE QUICKLY AND THUS AN IDEAL GETAWAY ROUTE AFTER A HEIST.

THE SECOND SWEDISH SPEEDBOAT HEIST

When two friends steal the Swedish crown jewels, everything that can go wrong does.

JULY 30, 2018 ★ *STRÄNGNÄS, SWEDEN*

DESCRIPTION

Typically, when you hear about the theft of a nation's crown jewels, you probably assume that such a crime would need to be committed by a sophisticated crew of thieves. While that might be true in the movies, often reality is much stranger and sillier. The theft of Sweden's crown jewels certainly fits into that category.

While many of Sweden's crown jewels are securely locked in museums or vaults fit for a king (or queen), the burial regalia of King Carl IX and Queen Christina was kept on display in the basement of Strängnäs Cathedral just outside of Stockholm. King Carl's crown jewels consisted of the king and queen's burial crowns, orbs, and scepters. It might seem unusual to keep such valuable treasure in a church basement, but this is fairly common throughout several churches across Europe. Many churches use

treasures and oddities like body parts (relics) that allegedly belonged to various saints to help draw crowds. Plus, Carl IX was not a particularly popular or good king. In fact, his body was exhumed years after his death for the sole purpose of taking his jewels for display.

At about noon on July 30, 2018, two men pulled up to the Strängnäs Cathedral on stolen black bicycles. Wearing black hooded sweatshirts and carrying backpacks, the men walked inside and immediately drew suspicion from other people in the church. Undeterred, the men went to the basement, where several relics from Sweden's history were displayed in glass cases. The men approached the glass case with the crown jewels, smashed the glass, and reached in to grab both burial crowns and a ceremonial orb.

With the crowns in hand, the thieves ran upstairs and out the front door, and then jumped back on their bicycles, riding to a dock on nearby Lake Malaren. Once at the docks, they dumped the bicycles and took off on a speedboat. They were pursued by police, who had been alerted immediately. Police scrambled boats of their own and a helicopter, but the thieves were far enough ahead of them to make an escape. This getaway was more due to the size of Lake Malaren than to the thieves' driving skills. The getaway boat actually broke down in the middle of the lake and the thieves had to get towed to shore by a Good Samaritan.

While the thieves managed to get away on the day of the crime, they were hardly competent criminals. Back at the crime scene, police discovered large amounts of blood in the display case, almost certainly from when the glass was shattered, as well as a blood trail leading up the stairs and to the docks There was also blood on the discarded bicycles.

KNOWN SUSPECTS

Almost immediately, police were able to match the DNA from the blood to twenty-two-year-old Johan Nicklas Backstrom. When brought in for questioning, Backstrom initially only admitted to stealing and supplying the bicycles and the boat, but he did later confess to the crime when his terribly weak alibis were discredited. Backstrom was sentenced to four-and-a-half years for the crime.

After Backstrom's arrest, police also arrested Martin Cannermo, who had recently been released from jail. While Cannermo didn't leave behind DNA evidence, he was identified by the man who had helped tow their boat to shore during the getaway. Cannermo was named as the second robber and received a lighter sentence of three years because he was instrumental in returning the jewels.

THE CASE TODAY

On February 5, 2019, the missing crown jewels were found, heavily damaged, in a garbage bin with the word "BOMB" spray-painted on the side of the bin. Police were able to pull DNA from blood on the jewels and confirmed that Backstrom was a match. It's likely that the jewels were eventually dumped by the thieves after realizing that they would be impossible to sell, but not before trying to pry out the loose stones and possibly sell at least those.

OPERATION ODESSA
We're going to need a bigger boat.

1991–1997 ★ RUSSIA; MIAMI, FLORIDA; AND COLOMBIA

DESCRIPTION

The Soviet Union's collapse in 1991 was an event unlike any other in history. While other governments and countries had fallen in the past, none had ever done so with a nuclear arsenal and some of history's most advanced weaponry. With no formal government left to control militaries, ownership of these stockpiles quickly became a gray area.

Within a few months, a group of three enterprising criminals flew into Russia to buy motorcycles in bulk to sell in the United States and to South American drug cartels. Before long, the cartels became interested in less conventional modes of transportation, and the smugglers began working with Russian Mafia connections to provide the cartels with military helicopters. While the smugglers were able to buy these helicopters for cheap, the cartels were willing to pay top dollar, as the vehicles allowed them to quickly move massive amounts of contraband wherever they wanted.

After purchasing several helicopters, the cartel reached out to the smugglers to purchase yet another military vehicle, only this time they wanted a submarine. The smugglers were dumbfounded by this request, but managed to find a Russian admiral who was willing to make the sale. Two of the smugglers went to Russia to inspect the sub, a Foxtrot-class submarine called Project 641 by the Soviets. The vessel was nearly three hundred feet long with ten torpedo tubes and would be capable of hauling over forty tons of cocaine in a single load. It ran on diesel, but the admiral assured the men that it could be converted to electric for silent running. Once they provided the cartels with sufficient proof of legitimacy, one of the men, known to his friends as "Tarzan," returned to the United States while the other stayed in Russia to work on logistics.

The former Soviet naval officers offered to sell the submarine for $5.5 million, plus a meager $600 to pay a crew to pilot the sub to Colombia. The third smuggler, a former Cuban spy, told the cartels that the submarine would cost over $30 million. When they balked at the price, he reminded them that its cargo capacity would pay for itself soon enough. Before long, he and the cartel had reached an agreement. The smuggler would take $10 million up front, and collect the remainder upon delivery.

Before the delivery could be completed, dozens of federal agents, who had been wiretapping the smugglers for months, sprang into action, arresting Tarzan while he picked up his daughter from school. After hearing about Tarzan's arrest, the former spy fled to Amsterdam with the cartel's $10 million; he had no intention of returning it. After finding out they'd been robbed, the cartel began staking out the smuggler's family. Rather than caring that his family was in danger, the smuggler devised a plan to try to steal the rest of the money.

He called the cartel and offered them a second submarine in exchange for meeting with him with $25 million. He arranged a meeting at the Madrid airport, telling the cartel he was sitting in a specific taxi, while he watched from a distance to see if they brought the money. Perhaps unsurprisingly, the cartel did not fall for his plan, and the spy watched as cartel members abducted the occupant of the cab he'd described before making an exit of his own.

KNOWN SUSPECTS

Ukrainian mobster Ludwig Fainburg, who went by "Tarzan" to his friends, was born in Odessa, Ukraine, before moving to Israel and then moving again to New York City, where he worked as an enforcer for the Mafia. Tarzan eventually moved to Miami at the suggestion of his mob colleagues. Once Tarzan arrived in Miami, he opened a strip club called Porky's. The building was the actual Porky's from the movie. Almost immediately, Porky's became a hub for criminals of all kinds, as did his other business, a Russian restaurant named Babushka. There was so much criminal activity at Babushka that the feds ended up bugging the restaurant booths permanently.

Before long, when criminal organizations in the area needed to get something done, they came to Porky's and asked for Tarzan. If the Colombian cartels needed help moving coke, they went to Tarzan. If the Russian mob needed a building burned down? Tarzan. If the Italian mob needed money laundered? Tarzan.

If Tarzan couldn't do it, he knew somebody who could. One of his connections was Juan Almeida, a Cuban playboy who built his reputation acquiring hard-to-find cars and taking care of boats. Many people would reach out to Juan before going to prison to hide their boats so they couldn't be seized, and then when they got out of jail, they'd find that Juan had sold their boats! But he was such a smooth talker that more often than not, he'd end up selling them a new boat instead.

Almeida quickly became known as "the guy" in Miami to handle anything transportation related, from cars to boats. He even sold airplanes sometimes. And if you had the cash, he could do whatever you wanted to the vehicles.

Together, Tarzan and Almeida sold tons of boats and cars. They began making money hand over fist, and then the Soviet Union collapsed. There were no laws, and only one rule: enough money could buy anything you wanted.

Tarzan and Almeida flew to Russia to buy some motorcycles from a factory outside of Moscow, and Almeida got the idea to rent a cargo helicopter to transport them back to the airport. When they called the airport to arrange the rental, they found out that renting this helicopter with pilots was going to cost about $500. They ended up renting ten of them and eventually bought 250,000 motorcycles from the factory for $200 each. They took the vehicles to Colombia and made about $3 million after the sales.

After getting back from Russia, Almeida and Tarzan reached out to one of their associates named Tony Yester, a Cuban spy turned drug runner. He was once arrested with forty-one passports and fled to South America. He used his skills to rise to the top levels of the Medellin Cartel and reported directly to Pablo Escobar. Tony also dealt in arms trafficking and was the kind of guy who would send postcards to federal agency offices whenever he was in a new place, just to mess with them.

One day, a few cartel reps went to the marina owned by Almeida, and asked him to build a few cigarette boats for them with some crazy speed and distance requirements. Almeida was able to upsell them the idea of jet engines on some of the boats, making each boat worth a few million dollars. As the men left, they saw brochures on Almeida's desk for helicopters that Almeida was in the process of fitting with the same turbine engines and asked if they could buy a few of these helicopters as well. The cartels reached out to Yester, knowing that he knew Almeida and Tarzan, and asked him to keep an eye on everything.

Once the three men had a plan to buy, transport, and sell the choppers, they flew to Moscow. They made a deal to sell them to the cartels for $1.5 million each and talked the Russians down to about $650,000 each. Juan went to Colombia to complete the sale, while Tarzan stayed in Russia to make sure the flight went off without a hitch.

Of course, there was a hitch. The Russian mob stopped the plane and held Tarzan hostage. When Tarzan's initial demands to be released failed, he decided to bluff his way to freedom and claimed to work directly for Pablo Escobar. The Russian mobsters seemed intrigued, so Tarzan offered to arrange a meeting with the Colombian kingpin, and the mobsters happily accepted. Tarzan called Almeida and told him that the Russians wouldn't release him unless they got to meet Escobar. Since they couldn't get the real Escobar to go to Russia, Almeida flew back to Russia himself and pretended to be the world's most famous drug dealer. Miraculously, this plan worked and the Russian mobsters released Tarzan and even apologized, while Almeida negotiated a deal with the Russian mob to distribute coke for him throughout the country.

Almeida went back to Cali Colombia and completed the sale. Before long, the cartel reached out to Yester and asked for another military vehicle, but this time it wasn't a helicopter. This time, the cartel wanted to buy a Russian submarine.

THE CASE TODAY

Tarzan was convicted in 1997 but received a light sentence in exchange for providing testimony against Almeida. He spent thirty months behind bars before being deported to Israel, where his family had immigrated in 1999. Thanks to a successful appeal and Tarzan rescinding his testimony after getting deported, Almeida served only eighteen months for his part in the sub caper.

In January 2017, Almeida was charged by the Drug Enforcement Administration with conspiracy to possess narcotics with intent to distribute. He was sentenced to serve six years in federal prison.

After years of hiding, Yester was finally arrested in 2019 while traveling through Rome to a wedding, on charges unrelated to the submarine. He is currently being held in Italy and claims that he spent all of the $10 million.

THE MOST BEAUTIFUL CAR EVER MADE

When the world's most beautiful car gets stolen, the investigation spans the entire globe.

MARCH 3, 2001 ★ *MILWAUKEE, WISCONSIN*

DESCRIPTION

The classic car collecting scene, like most scenes, has a few levels. You have your hobbyists that collect and restore classics like a '57 Chevy. Next, are the muscle car fanatics who collect cars like the 1967 Camaro or a '68 Mustang GT500. Then there are the European car collectors that seek classic Jaguars, Mercedes, and the Italian masterpieces by Ferrari and Lamborghini. These are the cars that even non-car people can appreciate.

There's another class of car collectors, though, and the machines they obsess over are more than just machines: they're pieces of history. These collectors seek out old European racers: the cars that belonged to iconic celebrities, like James Dean's Porche 550 Spider or Steve McQueen's Mustang from *Bullitt*. For these collectors, it's not enough to have a type of car; they need to own specific

models, even specific serial numbers. Minor details like a specific paint color or a special gas tank can make these cars exponentially more valuable than their more common peers. To get collectors of this caliber interested, cars need to be beautiful, rare, and iconic.

Maybe no car meets those three criteria more than the 1938 Talbot Lago T150C-SS. Known as the "Teardrop," this car was built for racing and featured a shorter wheelbase to facilitate tighter turns, and boasted a six-cylinder 3996cc engine that created an incredible (for the time) 140 horsepower. Built just outside of Paris, the Teardrops were as gorgeous as they were race-worthy, and many called this model "The Most Beautiful Car Ever Made." As for rarity? Only two were ever made with the 140-horsepower engine.

One of these Teardrops was

purchased by Italian race car driver and three-time Le Mans winner Luigi Chinetti. In 1939, Chinetti imported his Teardrop to the United States and quickly sold it to Tommy Lee, the son of a wealthy car dealership owner. After Lee's death in 1950, the car changed owners multiple times until 1967, when it was purchased by Roy Leiske, a Milwaukee factory owner. Leiske kept the Teardrop in the warehouse where he operated his business, Monarch Plastics, on Marshall Street.

The car sat idle in the warehouse for decades but following the tragic death of Leiske's son in 1996, Leiske began to devote himself to restoring the car. He became obsessed with the project, and soon had the car in pieces and surrounded by the parts he'd need to get it back to its full glory. Word of the project quickly spread through car collector circles, and soon the warehouse on Milwaukee's lower east side became a destination for serious car collectors from all over the world, including Jay Leno. Many of the admirers tried to buy the car from Leiske, but he refused to sell it.

Unfortunately, not all of the admirers had good intentions. Early in the morning on March 3, 2001, a team of three men cut the phone lines at Leiske's home—to disable security alarms and prevent Leiske from being able to call police—and pulled up to the warehouse. Next, the men used a trolley beam hoist attached to the warehouse's steel beams to lift the pieces of the car and move them from the back of the warehouse to the garage door. This hoist allowed the team to move quickly and extract the car without moving any of the obstructions that had blocked it in. Before long, the car parts were loaded into a box truck parked in front of the warehouse door. The thieves went back through the warehouse and searched various drawers and cabinets for all of the necessary paperwork and loaded up pieces from another Talbot that Leiske had been using for his restoration. Once the thieves had everything they needed, they drove off. At approximately 10:00 a.m., Leiske arrived at the garage to begin the day's work on the car and discovered that it was stolen. The Milwaukee police put the car into a local and federal stolen car database.

Neighbors reported seeing the car getting loaded into the truck by three men in overalls but had just assumed that Leiske finally got an offer on the car that he'd accepted.

The thieves immediately repainted the car and chassis. The car was moved out of Wisconsin and promptly hidden in storage in Oakland, California.

KNOWN SUSPECTS

In 2005, Roy Leiske died, leaving his second cousin, Richard Mueller, as his heir. Shortly after, he received a phone call from a man named Chris Gardner. While on the phone, Gardner asked about buying some of the parts from the remaining Talbot, and in October 2005, he traveled to Milwaukee and offered to buy Talbot outright. Mueller agreed, and sold it to him, giving Gardner a legitimate bill of sale for a 1938 Talbot with Mueller's signature on it.

Gardner used that bill of sale to forge ownership documents for the Teardrop, and then used those documents to have the Milwaukee police remove the car from the stolen car database. Amazingly, the Milwaukee police did not ask any questions or contact Mueller to verify

that he'd recovered and sold the car, and removed the car from the local database.

Gardner then had the car moved to Europe, pretended to be the car's owner, and began having it restored by a mechanic in the French Alps. The restoration was going off without a hitch until Gardner refused to pay the mechanic, which is probably the biggest cardinal sin in heists. Furious, the mechanic removed the original engine from the car, but Gardner was able to get another mechanic to put in a similar, but much less rare engine, and sold the Talbot to a buyer in Illinois for $7.6 million in 2015.

This purchase set off red flags though, as the car was still listed on the federal stolen car database. Authorities were notified, and soon

Mueller and his business partner, Joe Ford, were informed that the car had been located. When a forensic analysis of the vehicle was done, investigators were able to use acid to restore the original serial numbers and prove that this car was in fact Mueller's Teardrop. The French mechanic had also reached out to Ford and informed him that he'd kept the original engine and handed it over to authorities.

THE CASE TODAY

Currently, the car is the subject of an intense legal battle between Mueller and Ford and the car's new owner, Rick Workman. Mueller and Ford have been able to prove ownership of the engine, worth approximately $2.5 million by itself, but are arguing that the car is stolen property and rightfully theirs as well. Workman's lawyers are arguing that the sale was legitimate, and that Workman couldn't know that the car was stolen when he purchased it, which is a difficult argument to make when only two such cars exist in the world and one of them was pretty famously stolen. Until the case is settled, the car is being kept in a (hopefully) more secure garage outside of Boston.

THE SISI STAR HEIST

If you have the chance to skydive into a heist, you need to take it.

JUNE 1998 ★ *AUSTRIA*

DESCRIPTION

In the middle of the night in early June 1998, a small single-engine plane flew at a low altitude toward Austria's answer to Versailles, the Schloss Schönbrunn palace. Once the aircraft was as close as possible, a man jumped out of the plane and into the darkness. After activating his parachute, he quietly glided toward the palace and landed on the building's roof, nearly falling to the ground four stories below when his parachute caught wind and began pulling him over the edge. He was able to grab onto a railing and secure himself.

After removing his chute, he made his way to a window that he'd unlocked a few days earlier while on a tour of the palace, and climbed into the building. He made his way to a display case that held the palace's greatest treasure: the Koechert Diamond Pearl, also known as the Sisi Star.

Featuring an enormous pearl in the center of a ten-point star, with each arm of the star covered in diamonds, the Sisi Star was one of twenty-seven jeweled stars commissioned in 1865 by Empress Elisabeth I of Bavaria, nicknamed Sisi. Elisabeth often wore several of them in her hair at a time, though she did give away several of the stars as gifts to her friends and ladies-in-waiting. Elisabeth was assassinated in 1898, and currently only two stars remain, one of which was about to be debuted at Schloss Schönbrunn on the hundred-year anniversary of Sisi's death.

Though the display room had several motion detectors, the thief was able to bypass them by moving slowly enough to avoid setting off the detectors. Once he arrived at the Sisi Star's display case, he finished removing the screws in the case that he'd sneakily loosened with a dime during his tour. He carefully reached into his bag and pulled out a replica of the Sisi Star that he'd purchased from the gift shop, and swapped the replica out with the real Sisi Star. With the jewel secured, the burglar carefully replaced the display case, tightened the screws back to normal, and then carefully made his way out of the same window he'd entered, before rappelling down to the ground from the roof. He fled the palace grounds on foot, and disposed of his parachute and rappelling gear in a garbage can.

KNOWN SUSPECTS

Gerald Blanchard and his mother moved from Winnipeg, Manitoba, to Omaha, Nebraska, after she divorced his father. Blanchard got an early start as a thief. At age six, he stole milk from his neighbor's porch, because his family couldn't afford it. A few years later, while attending middle school, he was caught stealing a VCR from one of his teachers' classrooms, but rather than punishing Gerald, the teacher decided to take him under his wing and teach him home mechanics.

Gerald was innately gifted with his hands, and quickly picked up woodworking, automotive work, construction, model building; he was great at it all. He could take things apart and put them together incredibly efficiently; he just seemed to know how everything worked. Gerald's teacher became something of a father figure to him, but despite his best efforts at straightening him out, he recognized that Gerald was the kind of guy that would rather spend five hours cheating on a test than one hour studying.

As a teenager, Gerald quit his job stocking groceries because he realized he could make way more money selling stolen merchandise from department stores. He possessed an innate ability to zero in on employees that would help him out, and used this ability to make tens of thousands of dollars fencing this stolen merchandise.

Gerald pivoted from mechanics to electronics, and started learning everything he could about cameras, security systems, computers, and other equipment. When he was sixteen he emptied out an entire RadioShack on Easter Sunday, and then bought a house with $100,000 in cash for his mother through a lawyer that he hired to broker the deal. He told his mom that the home belonged to a friend and whether or not she believed him, she looked the other way.

After his first arrest, he was given

the shock treatment of jail to try to scare him into good behavior, but it didn't work and he continued to get arrested. On at least two occasions, his almost-supernatural ability to find weaknesses led to him escaping containment. One time, Gerald escaped through the ceiling of his interview room and even stole a uniform, badge, and gun on his way out. Another time, he slipped his handcuffs over his feet so his hands were in front of him and then managed to steal a police car. Eventually, he was deported back to Canada where he continued his criminal ways.

In 1998, Gerald, his wife, and her wealthy father took a grand European vacation. Over the course of six months, they visited Rome, London, the French Riviera, and several other destinations. While in Austria, they stopped at Schloss Schönbrunn, where Gerald's father-in-law's VIP status got them a tour of the palace and a special early viewing of the Koechert Diamond Pearl. During the tour, Gerald decided that he would steal the Sisi Star, and paid close attention to the security systems in place to protect the museum. Amazingly, he was able to not only open one of the windows in the showroom, but also used a dime to unscrew the display case's screws, making it easier for him to pull off the heist when he returned.

THE CASE TODAY

After the crime, Gerald headed back to Canada with his wife and father-in-law, stowing the $2 million hairpiece in his scuba tank. Knowing he'd be unable to sell it, he kept the star hidden in his grandmother's basement. Despite pulling off one of the most audacious heists in history, Gerald wasn't done. He launched what police called the "Blanchard Criminal Organization."

He began targeting ATMs, typically once he saw a new branch of a bank being built. Throughout the bank's construction, he would sneak onto the site, taking careful notes of how things were laid out, and what security mechanisms were being used. He then bought versions of his own to reverse engineer. Eventually, he could assemble a complicated ATM lock in under forty seconds. He got so good at breaking into the ATMs that he could be in and out of a bank within a minute and a half.

No matter what security measures came up, Gerald had a solution. He'd use IR goggles to see infrared beams, or lead-lined bags to block them. He learned to contort through air ducts. Sometimes, he'd build his own signal jammers or surveillance gear. He would take his money down to any number of his multiple Caribbean bank accounts, each set up with a different pseudonym.

In 2004, as a new branch of the Imperial Canadian Bank of Commerce was preparing to open in Winnipeg, he stole over half a million dollars from the freshly stocked ATMs. Police arrived within eight minutes of him opening the first ATM, but when they got there, they found only locked doors and assumed it was a false alarm. Gerald also left one of the ATMs untouched just to leave a little mystery.

Despite the heist going off without a hitch, he made one critical error on this heist. Somebody noticed a van outside the bank and reported it. The license plate was traced back to a rental car company that had rented the van to one Gerald Blanchard.

Once he was arrested, he pleaded guilty to sixteen charges of robbery and fraud in Canada and elsewhere on November 7, 2007. Blanchard took police to his grandmother's home and handed over the Sisi Star, which was returned to the museum. In exchange for his full participation in the investigation, Blanchard was sentenced to only eight years in prison. After his release, he began working as a security consultant under an assumed name.

THE AUSTRALIAN GOLD WAGON HEIST

It's a g'day to steal some gold

JUNE 15, 1862 ★ *NEW SOUTH WALES, AUSTRALIA*

DESCRIPTION

The later nineteenth century was an unsettled time in Australian history. The continent was transforming from a prison colony into a regular colony. The population exploded from 50,000 in 1825 to 1.15 million in 1861 and the economy grew with it. As farmers pushed out into the countryside as part of this expansion, gold was discovered and Australia saw a huge gold rush. Having a gold rush on an island full of convicts went about how you'd expect, and crime was rampant.

The atmosphere was similar to the American Southwest: lots of prospectors and bushrangers. Originally, the term "bushrangers" applied to escaped convicts that hid from the law, but soon the term became shorthand for people who took up robbery for a living and used the outback/bush as a base.

Most of the gold being mined was taken to mining towns, where it was weighed and sold. The trail was pretty well established for this transport. Typically, the gold would be loaded into a stagecoach and driven by a team of armed guards/troops.

One team of bandits learned that an armored coach was due to carry a large load of gold. They surveyed the route and found a choke point near Escort Rock, a geological formation of enormous granite rocks, many the size of houses or larger. Now that the plan was set, it was time to pull off the heist. The men dressed in red shirts and blackened their faces to hide their identities, and rode out into the bush.

When they made it to the ambush point, they split in half; four men hid behind a huge rock and the other four hid in a creek bed. Once the wagon reached the ambush point, the men jumped out and told the guards to stand down, yelling "Bail up!" The bushrangers expected the officers to surrender the gold, and on most days, the officers might have done this. On this day, however, the wagon was carrying seventy-seven kilograms of gold and ten bags of cash, making the whole haul worth about $4 million in today's money.

The guards weren't just going to hand that much money over! A gunfight broke out and eventually the guards were overpowered. Two guards managed to escape, but one of the guards had his testicles shot off and another guard was also hurt, though less critically. The gang tracked down the wounded men and tied them up. They loaded up the gold and took off, with some Aboriginal trackers and police hot on their trails. In order to escape, the thieves were forced to leave one of the pack horses behind with a lot of the stolen loot.

KNOWN SUSPECTS

In another time, Frank Gardner could have made a living as a handsome Edgar Allen Poe impersonator. He was born in 1830 in Rosshire, Scotland. In 1834, he emigrated to Australia with his parents. His family was made the overseers of several properties owned by Scottish businessman Henry Monro, who traveled on the same boat and began a relationship with Frank's mother, Jane. Frank was by all accounts a smooth talker. He had an athletic build, hazel eyes, and wavy brown hair.

In 1850, When Frank was about twenty years old, he worked as a stockman in Victoria. The job was grueling and paid poorly, so Frank decided to go into a life of crime, finding two accomplices to help him steal a team of horses. They stole several horses and planned on selling them in nearby Portland, but authorities were able to follow the horse tracks and arrest all three. Frank was tried under his real name, Francis Christie, and sentenced to five years of hard labor.

Five months into his sentence, he and his work team rushed their guards and managed to escape. Most of his fellow escapees were rounded up pretty quickly, but Frank traveled to New South Wales, where he may have joined a few crews that robbed a gold escort, but he was never arrested. He decided to change his name once

again to Frank Clarke, and in February 1854, he and another man named Prior were caught selling stolen horses at Yass. This time, he was sentenced to fourteen years, seven years for each charge. He served his sentence on Cockatoo Island in Sydney Harbor, which was essentially the Alcatraz of Australia.

In 1860, he was given a ticket of leave, a kind of parole, on the condition that he stay in Carcoar, a tiny town about 160 miles from Sydney. Frank almost immediately returned to a life of crime and stole several cattle with John Piesley, another bushranger he'd met on Cockatoo Island. Frank got into a gunfight with some troopers and was briefly captured, but managed to bribe his way into another escape.

Shortly after this escape, he began planning his biggest heist yet. He decided to go from stealing livestock to stealing gold.

One of these gold towns was called Forbes, one of the only towns in the remote Central West region of New South Wales. Gold was transported from Forbes to Orange, and then finally to Sydney.

Frank watched for weeks from a butcher's shop as gold was loaded onto wagons and taken out of town. The shop was just a front for him to sell stolen livestock. It was widely known that he was an outlaw, though most pretended not to know. Frank observed that every Sunday, around ten kilograms of gold, along with cash, was loaded up and guarded by four armed men.

He started putting together a crew, including Ben Hall, who would become one of Australia's most famous bushrangers. Hall's girlfriend's sister was sleeping with Frank, and the two men became friends. Hall was the handsome Paul Newman to Gardner's handsome Edgar Allen Poe. The rest of the crew, eight men in total, consisted of Dan Charters, Henry Manns, Alex Fordyce, John Bow, John O'Meally, and John Gilbert.

THE CASE TODAY

Before long, the press got word of the crime and shockingly, they sided with Gardner's crew. They romanticized the heist and people treated the gang like folk heroes, but this was short-lived and eventually the law caught up to most of them.

Two months after the robbery, Charters turned himself into the police as an informant, on the condition that he would receive a pardon. Hall was killed by police when a shootout erupted during a different robbery. Four men went to trial, but only Manns was hanged. John Bow and Alex Fordyce were sentenced to a life of hard labor, but were eventually released. Frank Gardner himself was sentenced to life in jail, but after eight years, he was released on the condition that he be exiled to the United States. He moved to San Francisco in 1874, opened a bar called the Twilight Star Saloon. Though nobody is sure what happened to him afterward, the two most common theories are that he either died penniless in 1882, or married a rich American woman and had twin boys before dying in 1904.

D. B. COOPER'S AIRPLANE HEIST

History's most notorious hijacker.

NOVEMBER 24, 1971 ★ *PACIFIC NORTHWEST, UNITED STATES*

DESCRIPTION

Few criminals have captured the imagination of Americans as much as D. B. Cooper. Perhaps some of the golden age mobsters like Al Capone or John Dillinger have come close, but nobody is quite as legendary as Cooper, partly because legends are all we really have of Cooper.

On November 24, 1971, a man calling himself Dan or "D. B." Cooper purchased a ticket aboard Northwest Orient Airlines Flight 305 from Portland, Oregon, to Seattle. Cooper was dressed in a black suit and white shirt and carried with him a black leather briefcase. He took his seat, 18E, toward the rear of the Boeing 727 and ordered a bourbon and soda while the other passengers boarded.

At 2:50 p.m., the flight departed Portland International Airport and began the thirty-minute flight to Seattle. Shortly after takeoff, Cooper passed a note to the nearest flight attendant, Florence Schaffner. Thinking that the note was just

another lonely businessman's phone number, Schaffner put it in her purse without opening it. But, according to journalist Richard Steven, Cooper leaned in toward her and whispered, "Miss, you'd better look at that note. I have a bomb."

Later, Cooper would take the note back, but Schaffner described it as being written by a felt-tipped pen with neat, all capital letters, saying that Cooper had a bomb in his briefcase. Once Schaffner read the note, Cooper instructed her to sit next to him, and then opened his briefcase for a moment. The glimpse was enough for Schaffner to see eight red cylinders attached to a battery with red-coated wires. Cooper closed the briefcase and listed his demands. He wanted $200,000 in "negotiable American currency" and four parachutes: two primary chutes and two reserve chutes. He also stated that he wanted a fuel truck standing by in Seattle to refuel the plane once it landed.

Schaffner went to the cockpit to inform the pilots that the plane was being hijacked and to relay Cooper's demands. When she returned to the rear of the plane, Cooper was wearing sunglasses. The pilots notified air traffic control of the situation, and the plane was put into a circular flight pattern over Puget Sound. The passengers were told that the delay was due to minor mechanical issues. The president of Northwest Orient immediately approved the ransom payment and authorities began getting the money together from local banks. If the response seemed well-rehearsed, it's important to note that during this time, a large number of airplanes were hijacked. In fact, 1961–1973 is often referred to as "The Golden Age of Hijacking."

Still, Cooper's calm demeanor set him apart from other hijackers of the era, and the flight crew noted that he was acutely aware of the area's geography, even correctly pointing out Tacoma from the sky. Cooper remained polite and calm throughout the entirety of the flight to Seattle and offered to request meals to be ready for the crew upon landing. He ordered a second bourbon and soda and paid his bill.

After two hours of circling Puget Sound, Cooper was told that his demands had been met. The money, a fuel truck, and four parachutes were waiting for him. Originally, McChord

Air Force Base had offered up four of their military parachutes, but Cooper rejected those and demanded civilian parachutes with manual rip cords from a local skydiving school instead.

Once the plane landed, Cooper ordered the pilots to taxi to a brightly lit and isolated section of the runway. Next, Cooper instructed the crew to lower all window shades to mitigate the threat of police snipers. Northwest Orient's operations manager, Al Lee, walked to the aft staircase in civilian clothes and delivered the parachutes and a backpack filled with ten thousand twenty-dollar bills, each of which had been photographed onto microfilm to track the serial numbers. Once the parachutes and money were on board, Cooper ordered all passengers and flight attendants off the aircraft.

As the plane refueled, Cooper laid out the next phase of his plan. He wanted the plane to fly him to Mexico City, but was adamant that the flight happen at the lowest speed safely possible, approximately 115 miles per hour. Cooper also demanded that the plane's altitude not exceed 10,000 feet and that the flaps be lowered to fifteen degrees with the landing gear remaining in takeoff position for the entire flight. He also requested that the cabin should remain unpressurized.

When the plane's co-pilot, William Rataczak, informed Cooper that this flight configuration would limit the plane's range to approximately 1,000 miles, Cooper and the crew discussed their options and decided to refuel the plane in Reno, Nevada, before continuing on to Mexico City.

Two hours after landing in Seattle, the plane took off for Reno with only Cooper, two pilots, a flight engineer, and one flight attendant. As the plane took off, two Air Force F-106 fighter jets followed, but stayed far enough back for Cooper to not notice. The Air National Guard also scrambled a T-33 that was in the area on an unrelated mission to follow the 727, until the T-33 ran low on fuel near the Oregon-California border.

Cooper ordered flight attendant Tina Mucklow into the cockpit with the rest of the crew and demanded that the cockpit door remain closed. Before entering the cockpit, Mucklow observed Cooper tying something around his waist. A few minutes later, at approximately 8:00 p.m., the rear staircase apparatus was activated, and moments later, the air pressure changed sharply, indicating that the rear staircase door had been opened. The crew used the in-plane intercom to ask Cooper if he needed assistance, but he refused any help.

At 8:13 p.m., the tail of the aircraft suddenly moved upward, and the pilots needed to manually get the plane back to a level trajectory. Two hours later, at 10:15 p.m., the plane

landed in Reno for refueling, but Cooper was not on board. Instead, police found his tie clip, his clip-on necktie, and two of the parachutes. One of the parachutes had its shroud lines cut, most likely so Cooper could tie the money bag to his body.

Authorities immediately began their investigation, interviewing witnesses in Portland, Seattle, and Reno, and police created the now infamous composite sketches of D. B. Cooper. Authorities traced the route of the 727 and began searching for clues on the ground, but the search area proved far too large and police were missing too many key data points—such as the amount of time Cooper spent in free fall before pulling his chute—to be able to narrow down the search area to a manageable size.

Flight tests would later show that Cooper almost certainly jumped at 8:13 p.m., but during that time, the plane was in the middle of a rainstorm, and conditions were too unpredictable to provide much meaningful data about where he could have landed. Only four pieces of physical evidence have ever been recovered, further complicating the case.

KNOWN SUSPECTS

During the investigation, over eight hundred suspects were interviewed, and police were able to narrow down their list of suspects to twenty-four, but were never able to conclusively prove that any of them were D. B. Cooper.

THE CASE TODAY

In November 1978, a set of instructions for lowering the rear staircase of a 727 were found by a deer hunter near Castle Rock, Washington. In 1980, an eight-year-old boy discovered three bundles of cash buried in a sandy riverbank of the Columbia River. The bills were still rubber-banded together and were proven to be 290 of the bills given to Cooper. No other money tied to the crime has ever been found or spent. In 2017, a nylon parachute strap and piece of foam that may have belonged to the money bag were found, but these claims have not been validated.

This case remains one of the most famous unsolved crimes in history.

HOT WHEELS

You've heard of car dealerships, but this is a car stealership.

CIRCA 1997–2001 ★ *NEW YORK CITY*

DESCRIPTION

When you hear about car theft rings, the first thing that probably pops into your head is the classic movie, *Gone in 60 Seconds*. In the film, Nicholas Cage and Angelina Jolie lead a team of thieves to steal fifty cars in seventy-two hours. Of course, the thieves couldn't just get normal cars; they had to steal luxury cars, sports cars, and classics on a gangster's wish list. The movie is fun, and it's based much more on reality than you might think.

Only, the real car theft ring wasn't filling one person's order; they were filling thousands of orders for wealthy buyers in China who wanted expensive cars that they couldn't legally import. Wealthy buyers would reach out to corrupt officials in the Chinese government and place an order for whatever kind of car they were after, and the order was sent to a team of thieves in New York.

KNOWN SUSPECTS

The leader of the New York operation was a man named Minjian Yang. Yang was born in China and served in the army as an intelligence officer. While in the army, Yang investigated and tracked down smugglers. Once he was out, Yang decided to take his skill set and start using it on the other side

of the law. He contacted members of the Chinese underworld and struck a deal: if the mobsters would support him, he would go to New York, create a team, and steal the cars.

Once Yang was given the green light, he moved to New York and created an identity for himself as a struggling immigrant named "Kenny." He found a dumpy apartment to set up operations in, and then brought in a trusted associate from Shanghai named Boy Chow to help manage the logistics and shipping operations. Yang and Chow began looking for a warehouse that they could use to move the cars. It was important that the location be away from police stations, in a quiet area, and not attract much attention.

Once Yang and Chow had their warehouse set up, Yang began recruiting car thieves through a man known only as "Dean." Dean in turn reached out to a master car thief named Mario Lopez. Mario's crew would handle the actual theft of the cars, while also providing for Yang and Chow a few layers of separation from the crimes. Mario's team of thieves was incredibly skilled and, just as important, disciplined.

Mario's crew would scout out driveways, garages, parking lots, and rental agencies until a car from the wish list was found. Due to their expensive nature, most of these cars featured sophisticated security systems; some would go off if they felt the car rock, while others had hidden GPS transponders. Almost all of them were computerized, a cutting-edge technology for the time.

The thieves were a step ahead, though. Rather than trying to break into the car via one of the doors and risk of setting off an alarm, they instead smashed the driver's side window. They'd then use the open window to connect the car's computer to a computer of their own. Once they were connected, they could send a factory reset command to the car's computer, putting it back in dealership mode and effectively disabling the car's security systems. The thieves could then unlock the doors and drive the car to an affluent neighborhood, where the car wouldn't seem out of place. Once there, they would perform a scan for GPS trackers and other anti-theft devices. Once any devices were removed, the car would stay parked for a cooling-off period.

After a few days, the thieves would go back to the car and be confident that the police were not looking for it. Then, during rush hour, one of them would drive the car to Brooklyn, parking it on the street a few blocks from Chow's warehouse. Next, Dean or Mario—the only two thieves that knew the actual location of the warehouse—would get in the car, and drive several laps around the block to ensure that nobody followed them, while a second car drove around a wider perimeter to be extra sure.

Once Yang was satisfied that the car wasn't being followed, he'd order Chow to open up the warehouse door. Chow and Yang had several boxes and pallets of food and restaurant supplies piled by the door to give off a legitimate appearance to passersby.

When cars entered the warehouse, Yang's team immediately went to work restoring them. Any damage done to the vehicle during the theft was fixed, locks were repaired, new keys were cut, and the car was detailed and cleaned to showroom condition.

Next, Yang used his smuggling expertise and connections to load the cars into overseas shipping containers, often building wooden platforms so he could stack cars on top of one another. Yang forged shipping documents from the warehouse that made it seem like the containers were carrying food and restaurant supplies. He made sure that each set of manifests carried an accurate weight for the container to avoid scrutiny, and then had the container trucks drive to New Jersey.

From New Jersey, the containers were loaded onto trains bound for the west coast before being put onto cargo ships destined for the East China Sea. Once the ship reached the East China Sea, a second cargo ship would intercept the shipment, take possession of the containers with the cars, and then replace the manifests with paperwork that accurately listed what cars were inside, doctored to make the cars seem legit, of course. Then, the cars were delivered to their new owners in China. On average, the entire process took around six weeks.

Yang and his crew turned car theft and smuggling into a science, and managed to steal and ship thousands of cars. After seeing the success of the operation, he decided to scale up and began targeting dealerships instead of individual cars. Yang and Dean had Mario test-drive cars at luxury dealers, making sure to note where the key lockboxes were located.

A few nights later, Mario and his crew would break into the dealerships, open the lockbox, and use the dealer keys to drive off with up to seven cars at once, cars that were already in showroom condition. Typically, the cars were gone in less than three minutes.

Unfortunately for Yang, one night after a dealership robbery, one of the drivers got into a car accident while exiting the Triboro Bridge. When police arrived at the scene, the car was identified as stolen and the driver was arrested. Once in police custody, the driver began offering information about Dean in exchange for a lighter sentence. Authorities opened an investigation into Dean and began surveilling the warehouse in Brooklyn, but Yang and Chow had employed countersurveillance that tipped them off to police presence. Yang and Chow cleaned out and abandoned the warehouse just ahead of a police raid and vanished.

THE CASE TODAY

The police kept a wiretap on Dean's phone, and after six months, Yang resurfaced. He called Dean and said that he was back in New York and looking to fill a big order for over 250 cars. Fearing that police were still listening to calls, Yang instructed his crew to swap phones and SIM cards often, but police were able to obtain the new phone numbers by tracking calls received by the thieves' wives and friends. Soon after, police raided the warehouse and then arrested Yang outside his home.

Yang was charged with the theft of several cars and pleaded guilty to corruption charges in exchange for a ten-year sentence. Police were unable to recover any of the approximately $40 million that they believe Yang earned for the thefts.

THE GREAT TRAIN ROBBERY

These thieves had a train to catch.

DESCRIPTION

Traveling Post Office (TPO) Trains, like the name implies, were trains that were specially purposed for delivering and sorting mail between stations, particularly in the United Kingdom. Equipped with special apparatuses to pick up or deliver mailbags without stopping, the trains became a vital tool in the timely delivery of post and valuables. Most TPOs even had a special high-value carriage that carried sensitive or valuable items or helped transport cash from one end of the line to the other.

The TPOs were effectively rolling fortresses, hundreds of tons of steel that barreled from one station to the next with no shortage of guards and locks to help safeguard their cargo. Despite being part of a larger train, the high value cars were generally off limits to anyone but approved staff and were typically located directly behind the main engine car.

Just after 3:00 a.m. on August 8, 1963, a TPO train headed from Glasgow to London was near the village of Cheddington. As the engineers rounded the corner and looked toward the signal light, which was usually green at this time of night, they saw a red light. The train rolled to a stop, but the signal wasn't changing. After a few minutes, co-engineer David Whitby exited the train to investigate. When he arrived at the signal, he discovered that the normal light had been covered with a leather glove, and that somebody had wired the red stop signal to shine with a series of wires and six-volt batteries.

As Whitby made this discovery, a man grabbed him from behind and told him that if Whitby screamed, he'd be killed. Approximately a dozen more men, all wearing ski masks, emerged from the dark and led Whitby back to the lead car of the train. Head engineer Jack Mills tried to fight the men off but was hit

in the head with a crowbar and began bleeding heavily from his wound. With Mills incapacitated, the thieves went to the back of the high-value car and detached the ten standard TPO cars behind it. As far as the approximately seventy-five postal employees on the last ten cars were aware, they were still just stopped for a delay, but unbeknownst to them, the lead two cars had started moving again.

Once the two lead cars had traveled just over a mile and a half from the rest of the train, they were told to stop the train once again over Bridego Bridge. Mills and Whitby were handcuffed together on the floor and told to keep quiet. The thieves entered the high-value car, and immediately overwhelmed the four

unarmed security guards. With the guards subdued, the thieves pulled out tools and began breaking open the steel door to the money room where 120 mailbags sat, full of mostly small bills. Once the door was opened, the thieves formed a human chain and began taking mailbags full of cash and throwing them down an embankment where they were quickly loaded into Range Rovers with matching license plates and a military-style supply truck.

Within fifteen minutes of stopping the train, the thieves had stolen 120 mailbags worth approximately £2.6 million, or $40 million in today's dollars. Once the money was loaded into the trucks, the thieves drove off, using back roads to get to their hiding spot: a property known as Leatherslade Farm, approximately thirty miles away, which they had purchased several months before the heist and used as a command center, complete with a police radio.

Back on the main train, one of the postal guards finally ventured out to see what was causing the delay. Upon seeing that the first two cars were missing, he ran to the nearest train station and called the police.

Cheddington police arrived at the crime scene and began canvasing the local area, looking for clues and searching databases of known criminals. Before long, they were joined in their efforts by Scotland Yard's Flying Squadron, a police team that specialized in robbery investigations. Police quickly realized that a heist like this would require someone to have inside knowledge of the TPO system, and of this route specifically. Somebody knew exactly where to stop the train, where to unload the cash,

and what day would yield the most cash; police were determined to find them. They suspected this individual was high ranking because they also knew that this particular TPO had not yet been equipped with new alarm systems that were being dispatched to trains all over the country.

For weeks, police searched the homes of known players in the underground, interrogated girlfriends of London's biggest thieves, and chased any lead they came upon. Finally, after over a month of fruitless searching, they received a tip from a shepherd that he'd seen some suspicious men around Leatherslade Farm. The shepherd said that he'd noticed a big increase in traffic around the usually quiet farmhouse in the days leading up to and after the heist. Police would catch another break in the case when an unidentified informant provided a list of eighteen names.

KNOWN SUSPECTS

Once the police arrived at the farm, they discovered twenty empty mailbags on the ground next to a deep hole and a shovel. Soon after, they found the getaway vehicles covered with tarps. Inside the farmhouse, they found pantries full of food and board games, and pulled fingerprints from

a ketchup bottle and a handmade Monopoly board, which they were able to link to Roger Cordrey, who worked as a florist in Bournemouth. Police would later discover that the thieves played the Monopoly game using the heist money.

With Cordrey arrested, police

were quickly able to arrest twelve more accomplices over the next few weeks by matching fingerprints to names on the informant's list. The heist's masterminds were quickly identified as Bruce Reynolds and Gordon Goody, as well as the inside man who was known only as "The Irishman" or "The Ulsterman."

Goody was a fairly well-known thief who'd famously been implicated, but later acquitted, in the 1962 Comet House heist. As the jurors of the Comet House case left the courtroom after declaring Goody innocent,

Goody approached the evidence table and showed the prosecution's forensics expert a false link that he'd put into the chain that allowed the robbers to escape.

Goody was arrested shortly after Cordrey, but Reynolds wouldn't be brought to justice until five years later, along with Ronald Edwards and James White. The other men arrested in the crime were: Charlie Wilson, Brian Field, Roy "The Weasel" James, John Daly, Henry Smith, Bob Welch, Tommy Wisbey, Jim Hussey, Danny Pembroke, and Ronald Biggs.

THE CASE TODAY

In total, fifteen men would be arrested and later convicted in the heist. Most of the men received sentences between twenty and thirty years. The identity of the Ulsterman has never been confirmed but shortly before his death, Goody told journalists that the Ulsterman was named Patrick McKenna. This has never been conclusively verified, and McKenna died poor and without being formally charged.

Ninety percent of the stolen money has never been recovered, but in 1971 UK currency was changed out, rendering the remaining cash in circulation worthless if it hadn't been spent by then.

THE FIRST AMERICAN TRAIN HEIST

No matter how good the plan, sometimes hings go off the rails.

JULY 21, 1873 ★ *ADAIR, IOWA*

DESCRIPTION

On the evening of July 21, 1873, a gang of bandits gathered in Adair, Iowa. After stealing a tie hammer and spike bar from a garage, the men went down to a curved stretch of railroad track a mile and a half outside of town. They worked quickly to remove the connecting plates for two pieces of rail, and tied a rope to the track. After running the rope into some nearby bushes, the thieves waited for their target to come around the bend.

Before long, the Chicago, Rock Island, and Pacific Railroad train came barreling down the tracks. The thieves had targeted this train line because it was frequently used to transport large amounts of gold, worth tens of thousands of dollars. As the train approached the thieves' hiding spot, they pulled on the rope and dislodged one of the sections

of track, derailing the train almost instantly and toppling several of the cars into the nearby Turkey Creek. One engineer and the train's fireman were killed in the rollover.

With the train now stopped, the thieves ran out of the bushes and boarded it. Once inside, the thieves made their way to the vault car, where they discovered that this train held only $2,000 in gold instead of the $75,000 they'd expected. Disappointed but not deterred, the bandits loaded the gold and then robbed the passengers of an additional $1,000 before exiting the train, mounting their horses, and riding off, having just completed the first train robbery in American history.

KNOWN SUSPECTS

Word of the robbery spread like wildfire, and almost immediately Jesse James and the James-Younger Gang were identified as the culprits. In order to evade capture, the gang split up and headed to several different states after the heist, but their reputation as the nation's most daring thieves continued to grow. Jesse would go on to gain infamy for his crimes, and to this day remains a legend of the Wild West despite operating primarily in the Midwest.

THE CASE TODAY

The James-Younger Gang was wanted almost immediately after the robbery, with rewards of up to $10,000 offered for their capture. Despite the high profile of the robbery, Jesse James would never formally be arrested or charged with this crime, though authorities would continue to chase the gang over the next several years.

THE SWEDISH HELICOPTER HEIST

In Stockholm, the only thing better than a boat is a helicopter.

DESCRIPTION

The G4S building in southern Stockholm is fairly unique. Only six stories tall, the building is topped with a giant glass pyramid, not unlike the one in front of the Louvre, which acts as a skylight. While the outside of the building looks fairly unassuming, inside lies one of the largest cash repositories in Sweden. The building served as Stockholm's central cash source for ATMs and banks around the city, and its formidable security kept thieves away. But just as the Death Star had a fatal flaw in its thermal exhaust ports, the G4S building had a flaw as well: the glass pyramid on its roof.

In September 2009, a team of thieves decided to exploit that flaw and came up with a plan for what is probably the craziest heist in Swedish history. They began studying streets around the depot and airports, timing how long it might take police to reach the building and what routes they

might take. After weeks of research, the team was ready to strike. It was important that they struck just before the twenty-fifth of the month, as that is the day in Sweden when salaries are paid out, and the banks would need to have lots of cash on hand to facilitate that.

In the early morning hours of September 23, the thieves went around the streets surrounding the depot and laid out steel caltrops. Once the roads leading into the depot were unpassable, the thieves traveled to the Roslagens helicopter base just outside of town. The team knew they'd be able to steal a helicopter from the base, but just as importantly, they knew that the police kept their helicopters in the same hangar. After breaking into the base, four men boarded their stolen Bell 206 aircraft and headed for the G4S building.

At 5:15 a.m., the helicopter landed on the roof of the G4S

building. The thieves exited the aircraft and used sledgehammers and explosives to shatter the glass pyramid. Once the glass was broken, the men used ropes to rappel into the lobby, and some of the crew fired submachine guns into the air to gather the approximately twenty employees that were working inside the building. Next, the thieves pulled out more explosive charges—magnetized soda cans filled with nitrate crystals—and began detonating them to gain access to the cages containing the cash.

Alarms went off almost immediately, and within ten minutes, the police at the helicopter base were called to action. The on-call pilots were scrambled to the helicopters but stopped in their tracks when they saw at least two plastic toolboxes with flashing red lights and a sign that said "BOMB" next to the fuel tanks in the hangar. The police called the bomb squad to investigate, but by the time they discovered that the bombs were fake, it was too late.

Back at the depot, the thieves moved quickly, getting as much cash as possible back up to the helicopter. Three of the men gathered cash, while the remaining man rounded up and kept watch on the employees, eventually getting them through an emergency exit on the sixth floor after one of the employees refused to open a vault in the basement. The thieves

put up a series of ladders and began moving the cash to the roof; one of the thieves was cut by the broken glass.

After only twenty-five minutes, the thieves returned to the helicopter and took off from the roof, before any authorities made it to the depot. The pilot reportedly dropped off a few of the passengers just outside of town, and then took off again, landing about an hour outside of Stockholm. There, the pilot and another crew member abandoned the aircraft in a meadow and left via speedboat. Despite the thieves having a substantial head start, the police caught up with them almost immediately. Within three hours, authorities located the abandoned helicopter and checked cell phone records from the time of the heist. Because the heist occurred early in the morning, there were not many records to sift through. Police quickly discovered a closed network of fourteen phone numbers that only made calls to the other phones in the network. None of the phone numbers made a call after the day of the robbery.

Now that police had narrowed down the number of phones used by the thieves, they were able to track the locations of these phones before and during the heist. Other investigators started running tests on the blood droplets found by the skylight and pulled DNA off the sledgehammer and the zip ties that the thieves used to secure the ladders. Police were getting close to a break.

Investigators began looking for the pilot. At the time of the crime, there were 552 people in Sweden with active helicopter licenses. Police ran checks against the pilot database and criminal databases, and then decided to narrow down the search a bit further by looking deeper into the registered pilots who flew out of the Roslagens base.

KNOWN SUSPECTS

Eventually, police discovered a pilot named Alexander Eriksson, a thirty-four-year-old TV producer who kept his own helicopter at the same base. Eriksson didn't seem like a likely suspect, though; he lived a pretty upstanding life, working a good job and raising his children with his ex-wife, whom he still lived with. Eriksson had a criminal record, but it was not the kind of record that a bank robber would have. He'd been arrested only twice in the past decade, once for drugs and once for a gun charge. Both were minor offenses, and he served no jail time.

When detectives pulled up Eriksson's address, however, they got a break they weren't expecting. The police had been running an investigation into a Montenegrin criminal named Goran Bojovic for an upcoming robbery, and during a surveillance session at the beginning of September, they'd seen a black Peugeot park nearby. The car's driver exited the car, shook hands with Bojovic, and left quickly after. When police ran the plates on the car, they found it registered to Eriksson's ex-wife. They didn't think anything of it until the address popped up again while investigating Eriksson, and now they had their first two suspects.

Police arrested Bojovic at his apartment and discovered a brand-new BMW and a duffel bag full of cash in his closet. The next morning, Eriksson tried to flee for the Canary Islands, but he was arrested by authorities at the airport. Within a few weeks, DNA from the blood spatters and explosive charges identified two more suspects: an Iraqi-born Swede named Safa Kadhum and Mikael Sodergran, who had previously been arrested on explosives charges. Ultimately, police would charge ten people in connection with the heist, and seven would be sentenced to prison.

THE CASE TODAY

In October 2010, the men went to trial. Bojovic, identified as the ringleader, was sentenced to eight years in prison. Eriksson and Khadum were also sentenced to eight years. Sodergran received five years for his part in the caper, and two men that falsified alibis received one to two years in prison as well. The exact amount stolen has never been revealed, though it is likely in the hundreds of millions of US dollars. The vast majority of the cash has never been recovered.

★ ★ ★

GET TO THE CHOPPER!

WHO: REDOINE FAID ★ WHEN: JULY 1, 2018 ★ WHERE: REAU, FRANCE

WHEN NOTORIOUS FRENCH THIEF REDOINE FAID WAS SENTENCED TO TWENTY-FIVE YEARS IN PRISON FOR HIS ROLE IN A BOTCHED 2010 ROBBERY, HE SHOWED THE WORLD THAT THERE'S NEVER A BAD TIME TO HAVE A CHOPPER. ON JULY 1, 2018, FAID WAS IN THE VISITATION ROOM OF A PRISON IN REAU, FRANCE, WHEN THREE ARMED MEN ARRIVED AT THE PRISON'S ENTRANCE DEMANDING HIS RELEASE. AS GUARDS MOVED TO HANDLE THE GUNMEN, ANOTHER TEAM OF ARMED COMMANDOS LANDED A HELICOPTER IN THE PRISON'S COURTYARD AND MADE THEIR WAY TO THE VISITATION ROOM. AFTER GRABBING FAID, THEY ESCORTED HIM TO THE HELICOPTER AND FLEW AWAY IN ONE OF THE WORLD'S MOST DARING PRISON BREAKS. FAID WAS ON THE RUN UNTIL OCTOBER 2018, WHEN HE WAS CAPTURED JUST NORTH OF PARIS. AMAZINGLY, THIS WAS NOT THE ONLY TIME FAID STAGED A DRAMATIC ESCAPE. IN 2013, HE USED EXPLOSIVES TO ESCAPE FROM ANOTHER PRISON. HE IS CURRENTLY BEING HELD IN A MAXIMUM-SECURITY FACILITY. FOR NOW.

CHAPTER 2

BANK JOBS

There's no more iconic a location for a heist than a bank. Between the enormous vault doors, security guards, and cameras galore, no other building is capable of getting the imagination going quite like a bank. That's why thieves are willing to do anything from robbing a bank in the middle of a war zone to digging a tunnel into the bank's vault from a flooded sewer system. If there's a way in, bank robbers will find it, because banks are the big leagues. After all, they're where the money is.

THE CLAY COUNTY SAVINGS ASSOCIATION ROBBERY

America's first bank heist.

FEBRUARY 13, 1866 ★ *LIBERTY, MISSOURI*

DESCRIPTION

On February 13, 1866, thirteen American gangsters rode up to the Clay County Savings Association in Liberty, Missouri. Two men dismounted their horses and entered the bank. One of them approached the cashier, a man named Greenup Bird, and asked him to break a ten dollar bill. As Bird opened the register, the robber pulled out a pistol and shoved it in Bird's face. The other man then jumped over the counter and pointed his gun at Bird's son, William, who was the only other person in the bank.

Both robbers kept their pistols trained on the Birds and ordered them to put all of the bank's money, including a tin box of government bonds, into a grain sack. In total, they stole a little over $60,000, which is a little over a million dollars in today's money. Once all of the money was in the sack, the thieves forced the two

Birds into the vault, closed the door, and ran out to their horses and the rest of the gang. The heist lasted less than fifteen minutes.

However, they didn't realize that just closing the vault door wasn't enough to lock it, so the Birds simply pushed the door open, then ran out after them yelling "ROBBERY!" Their shouts caught the attention of two nearby men, S. H. Holmes and George Wymore. Holmes and Wymore saw the gang, who fired their guns in the air in an effort to scare off any witnesses. One of the gangsters, a man named Arch Clements, fired a shot at Holmes, hitting his coat, but luckily missing his body. As Holmes and Wymore started running away, Clements shot at them again and killed Wymore. After Wymore was shot, the gang rode out of town and into history.

This bank robbery might seem simple, and it is, but it is actually the first daytime bank robbery in American history. Banks had always been targeted by those with criminal intent and, previously, other banks had been broken into when they were closed, but it wasn't until this heist that anyone had the idea to walk into a bank during working hours with the intention of stealing money.

KNOWN SUSPECTS

Jesse James was truly a prolific criminal. In a time of outlaws, he stood out as the most iconic. He and his gang, the James-Younger Gang, committed brazen robberies and heists all over the United States. Jesse James didn't just commit bank robberies, though, he literally invented them. Jesse's gang committed the first daytime bank robbery in American history.

Jesse cased the bank and planned the robbery for several weeks, but wasn't able to participate in the robbery itself, because he was still recovering from a nearly fatal chest wound he got just after the end of the Civil War. In his stead, Jesse sent in his two most trusted gang members: his brother Frank James and Cole Younger, who led the Younger gang.

THE CASE TODAY

A few days after the robbery, Jesse sent a letter to Wymore's family apologizing for his death, stating that he never intended for anyone to be hurt during the robbery. Because James wasn't yet famous, it's likely that this message actually came from him, and cements the fact that he had indeed

planned the robbery. Despite James's eventual fame, nobody was charged with the crime and the money was never recovered. Today, the Clay County Savings Association Building is listed in the US National Register of Historic Places and operates as the Jesse James Bank Museum.

THE BUENOS AIRES BANK HEIST

The heist of the century.

JANUARY 13, 2006 ★ *BUENOS AIRES, ARGENTINA*

DESCRIPTION

Just before noon on January 13, 2006, a group of thieves put superglue on their fingertips to help disguise prints, and donned costumes before walking into the lobby of Banco Río, in Buenos Aires. The first man entered the bank dressed up as a doctor, while a second thief came in wearing a ski mask. The two men pulled out realistic-looking toy guns and yelled for everyone to get on the floor.

Outside, another thief drove a stolen car into the parking garage beneath the bank with a new accomplice, known only as Luis the Uruguayan. The two men carried bags full of tools into the bank, and then locked the garage door, using the car as an extra barricade. They then joined the first two robbers upstairs.

Minutes later, another thief took a different stolen car and positioned it to look like a getaway car with its emergency flashers on. He filled the backseat with nails and spike strips

and oil cans, to help sell the idea that this was the getaway vehicle. Then, he entered the bank wearing a ski mask, a blond wig, a baseball cap, and sunglasses. His disguise was so good that one of the other thieves pulled a gun on him for a second until he realized who it was.

The men started working on their own tasks. One would handle the police, while two of them worked to wrangle the hostages. Another would go to the janitor's closet in the basement and let the tunnel man know that it was time for him to dig the last few inches of the tunnel and come into the bank through the closet's wall.

Once he was in, the tunnel man leaped into action and assembled a tool he called his "power cannon" to start tearing open safe-deposit boxes, working feverishly. As he cracked open the boxes, two of the thieves piled the loot into bags, while the rest of the team worked upstairs.

The robbers upstairs emptied cash drawers, one of the men acting as the ringleader. He called himself "Walter" and donned a fake moustache and yarmulke with his gray suit. When he was ready, they set up a plan to contact the police.

Police had been on the scene for several hours at this point, arriving just minutes after 12:38 p.m.

Not long after the police set their perimeter, the bank's security guard emerged from the front door. His gun's bullets had been removed and placed into his pocket. Ten minutes later, a second hostage was released. The hostage and the security guard described the situation for the police: there were twenty-three more hostages and five robbers inside, each thief dressed in an assortment of disguises.

Another ten minutes passed, and "Walter" emerged with a hostage. After getting a look at the police outside, Walter set the hostage free and headed back into the building. Police set up radios and contacted him. Police let Walter know that the bank was surrounded, but Walter warned them to stay back until the thieves were ready to give themselves up, unless they wanted another Ramallo situation (more on that later).

Over the next few hours, Walter and the police communicated via radio. Walter assured the negotiators that the hostages were being treated

well; the robbers even sang "Happy Birthday" to one of the hostages after discovering that it was indeed their birthday. Just after 3:00 p.m., Walter asked the police to get some pizzas delivered for the hostages. Once Walter ordered the pizzas, he went radio silent.

Meanwhile, in the vault, the tunnel man dismantled his power cannon after nearly ninety minutes of ripping open safe-deposit boxes and cleaned out the room. He assembled some fake bombs and dropped the bags of loot down through the hole. The thieves sprayed the room down with bleach and then threw hair clippings from a barbershop into the vault, to prevent police from determining which DNA was theirs. They then climbed down into the tunnel and moved a file cabinet over the hole, making the closet appear to be untouched.

The five men jumped into the lead Zodiac, using a towline to pull a second Zodiac that they'd thrown the loot into. When the engine flooded and wouldn't start, the men handed out paddles and the team began their escape. After rowing for about ten blocks, the thieves stopped under a manhole cover and started hoisting the bags up to the street using a rope ladder and a pulley that the tunnel man had installed a few weeks prior. Once things were loaded, they pulled up the rope ladder and allowed the

Zodiacs to just float down the tunnel to the river, knowing that when the tunnel man's rigged dams broke, the water would wash away their footprints as well. The men got into their getaway van and drove off.

After trying to get ahold of Walter or any of the other robbers for three hours, the police decided to make their move. At 7:00 p.m., a team of specially trained officers breached the door and entered the building. While police had prepared for a shootout with the thieves, they found nothing. The hostages were split up on three different floors and locked in conference rooms, but they were unharmed. Walter and his team were nowhere to be found.

As police made their way into the bank's basement, they discovered that over 140 of the bank's 400 safe-deposit boxes had been ripped open. Then they found a pile of toy guns wrapped up neatly with a note from the robbers that simply said, "In a neighborhood of rich people, without weapons or grudges, it's just money, not love."

KNOWN SUSPECTS

Fernando Araujo and Sebastian Garcia Bolster were two friends from the upper middle-class suburbs of Buenos Aires. One day, they started talking about heists on a lark, and eventually the conversation drifted to a notorious bank heist that had happened a few years earlier in the town of Ramallo.

During the Ramallo heist, a group of robbers entered the bank. The police surrounded them, and eventually a shootout erupted. Police managed to kill one of the robbers, but in doing so, they'd also killed two hostages. The Ramallo heist was a national scandal and tragedy, and Fernando thought there must a better way to do things. He said as much to Bolster, and described how he'd do it if he could; the two laughed it off.

Fernando taught karate to pay his bills when he wasn't growing his own strains of marijuana. He was an artist and a big outside-the-box kind of thinker. He spent most of his time getting high and watching heist movies. At some point, he switched to watching documentaries and started plotting out what mistakes other robbers had made.

Bolster, on the other hand, was more mechanically inclined. He worked on small engines, repairing motorcycles and jet skis, and tried to come up with plans to build a cheap helicopter in his backyard. He tended to be more of a rule follower and a family guy.

A few weeks after their conversation about heists, Fernando went back to Bolster and told him that he needed him to build some technical gadgets for him. Bolster again said that he wasn't comfortable doing any kind of crime, but he did have a deep hatred of financial institutions, even though he'd been named the employee of the month at a bank he worked at part time. Hating banks was something of an Argentine national pastime; many of the country's banks suffered terrible crashes and cost people their entire fortunes, including Bolster's father and grandfather. He made Fernando an offer: if he could promise that there'd be no weapons or violence, then he'd help build his gadgets.

The men started putting together their plan: they'd utilize the vast underground sewer tunnels to dig under the bank. They knew they'd need to get around the bank's alarms, but they had a surprisingly simple solution to that: they'd just pull off the heist during working hours when the alarms were turned off.

They knew that they couldn't do this alone, so they reached out to some notorious thieves and brought them into the crew. Among the first to join was a duo of older criminals named Doc and Beto. Doc and Beto had worked together over several decades as part of one of Argentina's most infamous bands of thieves. As they started working on the plan above ground, Bolster started working on what to do below. Bolster spent his nights driving to Peru Beach and parking next to the giant opening where the city's storm drains emptied into the Rio de Plata. He'd walk in through the opening each night and spend the next thirty minutes getting as close as he could to the bank. From there, he used a hydraulic shovel to dig away at the dirt, moving at a slow but steady pace.

Bolster was very talented and used his smarts to solve problems as they came up. He was able to figure out the exact angle to dig by measuring out two sides of a triangle and then doing the math to get his angle. They'd be coming into the bank at an angle of sixty-nine degrees, steep, but doable.

As construction continued, the team started running out of money. Fernando sold his truck to help finance some equipment, but before

long, they needed to bring in an investor of sorts. Luckily, Doc knew just the guy, a Uruguayan thief named Luis Sellanes. He was a thief with a penchant for unconventional entry into buildings and had earned his nickname "The Spiderman of Buenos Aires." After hearing the plan, he was immediately interested and provided around $100,000 in funding and offered advice wherever he could.

With the tunnel nearly complete, Bolster realized that there was no way they'd be able to escape on foot with as much loot as they were anticipating. He came up with the idea of using Zodiac rafts. Unfortunately, the water in the drains rarely reached the depth the inflatable boats needed to operate safely, but Bolster had an idea for that too. He'd flood the tunnels using a series of dams.

Fernando looked at the plans from a top-down approach and began anticipating possible problems. Any time he saw a chance for failure or capture, he tried to build in a plan to prevent it; Sellanes and Doc helped him with this. Finally, the time came to put the plan into action.

THE CASE TODAY

The day after the heist, Bolster took many of the credit cards from the safe-deposit boxes and scattered them around various parts of the underground tunnels, all in locations far from their actual egress point. With the credit cards gone, the rest of the haul was reported to be approximately $20 million, but likely went into nine figures, due to safe-deposit box contents being notoriously underreported, especially in a country like Argentina, which saw thousands of Nazis arrive following World War II. The gang split up the money, giving Bolster, Fernando, Beto, and Sellanes the largest shares, with the late joiners getting a smaller cut.

For a few weeks, things were perfect. The police had no leads, and the nation was enamored with the "heist of the century. Then, Beto went for a drive with his girlfriend, and got pulled over for speeding. His girlfriend, angry that Beto had cheated on her, told the police about his involvement in the Banco Río job. Before long, the police were able to get the rest of the crew members, Fernando, Bolster, Sellanes, and Doc.

Sellanes was able to take advantage of a loophole that allowed non-Argentine nationals to only serve half their sentences if they got deported, so he ended up only serving four years.

Bolster got the lightest sentence as they only convicted him of the tunneling. He served just over two years in jail. He's still friends with Fernando, who helped consult on a movie based on the crime called *The Heist of the Century*. Most of the money was never recovered, and Argentina's short statute of limitations means that it likely never will be.

THE BILLION-DOLLAR BAGHDAD HEIST

When your dad's face is on the money, you can get away with this.

MARCH 18, 2003 ★ *BAGHDAD, IRAQ*

DESCRIPTION

Early in the morning of March 18, 2003, the day before the United States launched its opening assaults of the conflict (Operation Iraqi Freedom), three large trucks approached the Central Bank of Iraq. A man exited one of the trucks and delivered a handwritten note to the governor of the bank. The governor read the note, saw the signature at the bottom, and opened the vault doors.

Over the next several hours, a steady stream of metal boxes (each containing approximately $4 million) were loaded into the trucks. By the time the trucks were loaded, over $900 million in US hundred-dollar bills and over $100 million in Euro notes were taken from the bank. In the span of just a few hours, the thieves pulled off the largest bank heist in the history of the world—almost a quarter of Iraq's physical currency reserves—and they'd done so without firing a single shot.

KNOWN SUSPECTS

Of course, not just any thief can walk into a country's central bank and make a billion-dollar withdrawal with a note. In this case, the heist was pulled off by Qusay Hussein, son of Iraqi dictator Saddam Hussein. The note said simply that Saddam wanted to prevent this cash from falling into foreign control, and that it would be safer in his hands. Knowing better

than to refuse an order from Saddam, the bank governor stepped aside.

Once the money left the bank, the metal boxes were taken to several of Saddam's palaces for safekeeping. As the US troops pushed further into Iraq, stashes of the cash were found all over the country, as well as $650,000,000 that was found behind the walls in the palace of Saddam's other son, Uday. That cash, it would turn out, was not connected to the Central Bank heist.

THE CASE TODAY

As these huge amounts of cash were discovered by coalition forces, the money was quietly flown to Kuwait where it was counted and stored by US military officials. It was important to get the money out of Iraq as soon as possible to reduce the likelihood that it could be used to finance insurgent forces. This was only the beginning of the stealing, though.

Rather than returning the money to its rightful owner, the Iraqi Central Bank, the US military instead decided to use the cash to finance operations in the war as commanders deemed appropriate. This cash, as well as billions of dollars in other cash that had been airlifted into Iraq, were quickly distributed to forward operating bases, given to allies, and, of course, stolen by the military personnel charged with safeguarding the stash.

Soldiers stole stacks of cash regularly; some soldiers filled rucksacks with the stolen money, and others mailed it home or hid it in their gear before returning home. Eventually, this theft was so rampant that the FBI opened an investigation into the missing cash. They quickly discovered a series of deposits in Arizona made by US Marine Corps major Mark Fuller that totaled over $440,000. US Army captain Michael Nguyen, who had been in charge of dispensing the cash throughout Anbar Province, had stolen nearly $700,000 and was caught when he tried to purchase several new vehicles, including a BMW and a Hummer, in cash.

In total, nearly three dozen US service members would be charged with thefts related to this cash. Almost all of the cash from the original heist has made it back into circulation, and most of it is still out there today, possibly even in your wallet.

A NOTORIOUS NE'ER-DO-WELL
The man who sold the Eiffel Tower. Twice.

WHO: VICTOR LUSTIG
WHEN: 1890–1947
WHERE: EUROPE AND THE UNITED STATES

CRIMINAL LEGACY

If there were ever a Mount Rushmore of con artists, Victor Lustig wouldn't just be on it, he'd sell it to you. Born in 1890 in Austria-Hungary, Lustig became an accomplished gambler in his late teens but his criminal prowess also extended to forgery, counterfeiting, and his true calling, confidence tricks. Lustig's ability to combine these talents made him a criminal mastermind whose scams and grifts literally changed the way the world operated and nearly toppled the United States economy. He was so smooth and audacious a con man, he once scammed Al Capone out of $5,000 just for fun.

KNOWN HEISTS

After leaving school in Paris, Lustig began booking trips on ocean liners from Paris to New York City and back, where he often posed as a

Broadway musical producer who pitched nonexistent shows to the wealthiest passengers on board and turned many of them into eager investors.

When World War I erupted in Europe, Lustig traveled to the United States and began robbing banks by selling them their own bonds for repossessed properties. After Lustig made the sales, he would perform a quick sleight-of-hand trick and leave with the cash and the bonds, which he would use to sell again.

One of Lustig's most infamous scams was simply called "The Money Box" or the "Romanian Box" scam. Lustig gathered investors and showed them a wooden box he claimed was capable of reproducing any currency placed inside it within a matter of hours. Lustig would then solicit a large bill from one of the investors and insert it into a slot in the box along with blank paper, before adjusting a series of levers and dials on the side of the box. After waiting for the prescribed time, Lustig would open a chamber in the box that he'd previously filled with counterfeit bills and insist that the machine had just duplicated thousands of dollars in new bills.

Lustig would then sell the box to the highest bidder in the room, often for thousands of dollars. To ensure he had enough time to make a getaway,

Lustig would fill the secret drawer with several real currency notes to make the mark believe that the machine did in fact work.

While the Romanian Box did not actually print money, Victor Lustig was a prolific counterfeiter. Over a period of several years, Lustig produced so much counterfeit US currency that his "Lustig money" caused actual inflation in the American economy and reduced confidence in the authenticity of all money in the United States.

In 1925, Lustig returned to Paris to perform his most audacious scam. After looking at a newspaper, Lustig saw an article lambasting the Eiffel Tower for its expensive and frequent maintenance. Lustig created counterfeit French government stationery and sent letters to several of the area's largest scrap dealers, inviting them to a secret meeting at a fancy hotel. When the scrap dealers arrived, Lustig played the part of a deputy director general and told the men that upkeep on the Eiffel Tower was becoming too costly and public sentiment was increasingly shifting toward the landmark being seen as an eyesore. As a result, the Eiffel Tower would be torn down and sold for scrap.

He managed to get several of the scrap dealers to make a bid, and even successfully solicited a bribe from one of them. As this man seemed the most desperate, Lustig informed him that his bid had won, and collected payment of 70,000 francs (just over $1 million in today's money) before promptly fleeing the country to Austria. When the mark had proven to be too embarrassed by the scam to report the con to police, Lustig returned to France and sold the Eiffel Tower for a second time.

* * *

THE TEN COMMANDMENTS OF CON MEN, ACCORDING TO VICTOR LUSTIG

1. BE A PATIENT LISTENER. IT'S THIS, NOT FAST TALKING, THAT GETS A CON MAN WHAT HE WANTS.
2. NEVER LOOK BORED.
3. WAIT FOR THE MARK TO REVEAL POLITICAL OPINIONS, THEN AGREE WITH THEM.
4. LET THE MARK REVEAL RELIGIOUS VIEWS, THEN HAVE THE SAME ONES.
5. HINT AT SEX TALK, BUT DON'T FOLLOW UP UNLESS THE MARK SHOWS A STRONG INTEREST.
6. NEVER DISCUSS ILLNESS UNLESS SOME SPECIAL CONCERN IS SHOWN.
7. NEVER PRY INTO A PERSON'S PERSONAL CIRCUMSTANCES; THEY'LL TELL YOU ALL EVENTUALLY.
8. NEVER BOAST. JUST LET YOUR IMPORTANCE BE QUIETLY OBVIOUS.
9. NEVER BE UNTIDY.
10. NEVER GET DRUNK.

THE NORRMALMSTORG HEIST

The heist that coined the term "Stockholm Syndrome."

AUGUST 23–28, 1973 ★ STOCKHOLM, SWEDEN

DESCRIPTION

On the morning of August 23, 1973, an escaped convict named Jan-Erik Olsson walked into the Sveriges Kreditbank in Stockholm's Norrmalmstorg Square with a jacket draped over his arm. After waiting in line for a few minutes, he dropped his jacket and revealed a submachine gun. He fired shots at the ceiling, screaming, "The party has just begun!" in American-accented English.

While Olsson had initially planned on a quick robbery, the scene rapidly spiraled out of control; almost immediately, one of the bank tellers activated the silent alarm and police arrived. As one of the police officers entered the bank, Olsson opened fire and wounded him. The bank was now surrounded by police with Olsson and four bank employees stuck inside.

After realizing that this robbery was now a hostage situation, Olsson made his demands: $700,000 in cash, a getaway car with a full tank of gas, and the release of one of his accomplices, Clark Olofsson, from prison. Police responded quickly and within a few hours, they had delivered a blue Ford Mustang, the ransom money, and Olofsson, whom police sent into the bank.

Olsson demanded to be able to leave the bank with the hostages to ensure his safe passage, but police refused this request, leading to a standoff. Police had cut the bank's phone lines but managed to get another—monitored—phone into the bank to allow for communication with Olsson and Olofsson, and to allow the hostages to contact their families.

Outside of the bank, news crews appeared and began filming next to the police, with cameramen and snipers both trying to get clear shots. The crisis quickly became an international sensation, and the Stockholm police department was bombarded with callers offering solutions for ending the standoff that ranged from releasing angry bees to sending in the Salvation Army band to perform a concert of religious hymns. These ham-fisted responses did little to calm the nerves of the hostages or instill a sense of trust in the authorities.

Inside the bank, things seemed considerably calmer. Olsson and Olofsson moved the hostages into the vault to have a more fortified position. When one of the hostages, Kristin Enmark, began to shiver, Olsson wrapped his jacket over her shoulders. Another hostage began crying when her family couldn't be reached via the police telephone, and Olsson consoled her and encouraged her not to give up trying to reach them. Olsson allowed one of the hostages who felt claustrophobic in the vault to walk around outside of it, albeit on a rope leash. Olsson even comforted one of the hostages when they had a nightmare.

As the hostage situation continued over the next few days, the hostages and the captors started addressing each other on a first-name basis. Enmark even used the phone to contact Sweden's prime minister to beg him to allow Olsson and Oloffson to take the hostages with them in the getaway car, claiming that they were only scared of violence from the police and that Olsson and Olofsson had been treating them all very kindly.

When Olsson told the hostages that he may need to shoot one of them in the leg to let police know he was "serious," the hostages praised him for only wanting to shoot a leg, hoping that praising him would keep them within his good graces.

On August 26, while the hostages and their captors were bonding, police drilled a hole into the top of the vault from an apartment above the bank. They were then able to get photographs of the hostages and the robbers inside. When Olsson discovered the hole, he fired his gun into the air and threatened to kill the hostages if police attempted any gas attacks.

However, on August 28, the sixth day of the hostage crisis, police did just that and dropped tear gas into the vault. An hour later, Olsson and Olofsson surrendered, but when police tried to extract the hostages, they demanded to stay in the vault unless Olsson and Olofsson were first to leave so they could be assured that their captors would be safe.

When the hostages' demand was accepted, the captors and the hostages approached the vault door together and exchanged handshakes, hugs, and kisses until police apprehended Olsson and Olofsson. Even as the hostages were being loaded into ambulances, they cried out for their captors' safety and promised to see them again.

THE CASE TODAY

Olsson and Olofsson were both convicted and sentenced to prison for the robbery, but Olofsson was able to successfully appeal his conviction by claiming that he had only helped Olsson in order to ensure the safety of the hostages. Olofsson and Enmark visited each other often after the robbery and their families became close friends. Olofsson would later be arrested again for various other crimes.

Olsson served a ten-year prison sentence for the robbery but became something of a sex symbol and regularly received letters from fans who found him attractive. Eventually, Olsson married one of the women who regularly wrote to him. After his release, he committed a series of financial crimes and went on the run for over a decade. Then, when Olsson tried to turn himself in, police told him that they were no longer pursuing charges for those crimes.

The relationship between the captors and their hostages became famously known as "Stockholm Syndrome." To this day, the case has been referenced in countless movies, TV shows, and other media, though many portrayals of "Stockholm Syndrome" rely on the trope of the captors being smooth, trustworthy antiheroes who foster deep connections with their victims. In reality, the Stockholm captives developed trust for their captors because the police repeatedly bungled their responses to the crisis and left the criminals looking like the responsible adults. Even the psychologist who coined the term "Stockholm Syndrome," Nils Bejerot, failed to do even the most basic due diligence of interviewing the hostages after the robbery. While Stockholm Syndrome will likely be a mainstay in fiction, it is losing significant ground as a diagnosis in psychological circles.

THE DUNBAR HEIST

Why rob one armored car when you can rob all of them?

SEPTEMBER 13, 1997 ★ *LOS ANGELES, CALIFORNIA*

DESCRIPTION

Allan Pace III was a notorious joker at the Dunbar Armored Car Depot in Los Angeles, California. Pace worked as the facility's regional safety director, and his job duties required him to constantly tour the building and identify potential hazards. For a guy like Pace, this job had its advantages; he got complete access to the entire facility, home to one of the largest cash handling operations in the city. Pace's job also required him to photograph safety violations, so it wasn't unusual for him to walk around taking photos of anything that might catch his eye.

While he went around checking fire extinguishers, Pace also took notes about the location of security cameras and how they panned the rooms. He began perfecting his timing, and, before long, he could tour the entire facility without being captured on camera once. After a while, he began to think that robbing it could be possible.

He reached out to five of his life-long best friends and ran it by them, half-joking about it as a hypothetical scenario. His friends laughed but also didn't think it was unrealistic. Still, they just assumed he was joking, but as the night went on, they agreed that if they ever did pull off the heist and any of them were caught, they'd never give up the rest of the group. Pace even brought out copies of blueprints of the facility.

Pace was known for his practical jokes and sense of humor. His favorite prank was disconnecting taillights on forklifts and then joking about having to write up the drivers. Despite his antics, he was well-liked at the depot, and he even dated one of the security office's heads briefly, but the relationship didn't work out.

Unfortunately, Pace's relationship with Dunbar wouldn't work out either, for after pulling his taillight prank one too many times, he was fired on September 12, 1997. The following day, he and his friends leaped into action. The six men—Pace, Erik Boyd, Eugene Hill Jr., Freddie McCrary Jr., Terry Brown Sr., and Thomas Johnson—first went out to a house party in Long Beach, making sure that they were seen and heard partying. After spending a few hours at the party, the men left and changed into dark clothes and ski masks, armed themselves with pistols and shotguns, and headed to the depot just after midnight.

Using one of the keys that Pace hadn't turned in after leaving, the men entered the depot through a side door. They avoided detection because they were able to hide behind a Dunbar employee's large truck that Pace had

ordered to be parked along the side of the building during a safety inspection weeks earlier. Once they were safely inside, Pace guided the group to the facility's break room, ensuring that they avoided detection by the panning security cameras as they crossed through rooms and hallways. They arrived at the break room just before 12:30 a.m., and Pace knew that the depot employees would be entering the break room one at a time to take their breaks.

As each worker entered the break room, the thieves subdued them and tied them up with duct tape before they could activate the alarms. Pace knew the vault would be unlocked due to the large amounts of cash

coming in that night, and he had the keys to access the room containing the vault. Once the employees were subdued, the men made their way to the vault prep room, which was protected by an unavoidable security camera and two armed guards. Pace and his crew rushed the guards and subdued them as well, threatening to shoot them if the guards didn't sit silently and stare at the floor. One of the thieves guarded the tied-up men, while another opened the facility's bay doors to allow Hill to enter in a rented U-Haul truck, which he backed up to the loading bay.

Over the next thirty minutes, Pace located the bags that carried the largest denominations of nonsequential bills, and the team loaded up the truck as quickly as possible. Once Pace had determined that all of the most valuable bags had been taken, he went to the security room to get the surveillance tapes. His ex-girlfriend in the security department had mentioned that there was a second set of tapes hidden in a hallway closet, and he grabbed those as well. With all of the evidence of their heist bagged up, the crew left the facility. In just under an hour, they'd stolen $18.9 million—the largest cash heist in history—without firing a single shot.

The men changed back into their normal clothes and made their way back to the party to celebrate and solidify their alibis. The next day, police began their investigation. Pace was a natural suspect, but police were not able to find any conclusive evidence, and his alibi was verified by several people. The police did find a small piece of plastic at the scene that would later be identified as part of the taillight from a U-Haul, but because Pace didn't rent the truck, they couldn't link him to the crime. Instead, they decided to keep an eye on him to see if he started spending large amounts of money.

Pace and the gang were patient though and waited over six months for things to cool down. Then, the thieves split up their haul and examined the bills. During this time, they discovered that some of the bills were sequential, so Pace ordered them to be burned. They decided to launder the rest of the money in Las Vegas. After literally running the money through a washing machine to make it seem weathered, the men gambled until all the bills had been exchanged with clean ones.

The thieves started buying property and investing in real estate around Los Angeles, and they started a company called Extreme Entertainment that rented jet skis and party supplies, while also paying themselves generous salaries. Pace was so careful about money getting traced to him that he didn't even set up a bank account.

THE CASE TODAY

The crew did a good job of avoiding suspicion until Hill tried to purchase a home in cash that still had the original Dunbar bands. When the realtor notified police, Hill was immediately arrested. After telling Hill that they had his U-Haul rental form for the truck with the broken taillight, he flipped to get a lighter sentence, turning in the other five members of his crew.

Pace was arrested and refused to incriminate his friends. He was found guilty and sentenced to twenty-four years in prison. The other crew members pled guilty and received sentences between eight and seventeen years each for their parts. Police have only managed to recover $5 million of the stolen money.

★ ★ ★

THE AMERICAN ARMORED CAR ROBBERY CAPITAL

WHAT: ARMORED VEHICLE THEFT ★ WHEN: 1970–PRESENT ★ WHERE: HOUSTON, TEXAS

AUSTIN MAY BE THE OFFICIAL CAPITAL OF TEXAS, BUT THE ARMORED CAR ROBBERY CAPITAL IS DEFINITELY HOUSTON. DUE TO THE CITY'S NETWORK OF OPEN FREEWAYS, WHICH ALLOW QUICK ESCAPES, PLUS TEXAS'S LAX GUN LAWS, HOUSTON IS SEEN AS THE PREMIER DESTINATION FOR ARMORED CAR HEISTS. IN 2019, 50 PERCENT OF ARMORED CAR ROBBERIES IN THE UNITED STATES HAPPENED IN THE HOUSTON AREA, MOST OF WHICH WERE PULLED OFF BY LOCAL CRIMINALS WHO ARE FAMILIAR WITH THE CITY'S LAYOUTS AND THE TRUCK ROUTES. ALTHOUGH ARMORED CARS AND TRUCKS ARE TARGETED FOR LARGE AMOUNTS OF CASH, GOLD, AND OTHER VALUABLES THEY TRANSPORT, THE TRUCKS FREQUENTLY HAVE MUCH SMALLER HAULS THAN EXPECTED, WITH MANY ROBBERIES YIELDING LESS THAN $5,000.

THE BRITISH BANK OF THE MIDDLE EAST HEIST

High risk, high reward doesn't get more literal than robbing a bank in a war zone.

JANUARY 1976 ★ *BEIRUT, LEBANON*

DESCRIPTION

In January 1976, a team of eight men dressed in camouflage and protective gear stood in front of the Bab-Idriss branch of the British Bank of the Middle East (BBME) in Beirut. Each was carrying an M16 rifle equipped with an M203 40mm grenade launcher and high caliber pistols. If they looked like they were dressed for a war zone, it's because they were; the Lebanese civil war had been raging on for nearly a year at this point and would continue for over a decade. Most of Beirut had lost its electricity, and the constant fighting between various religious and political sects meant that the sounds of gunfire and explosions were constantly ringing out.

The BBME was located in the middle of the so-called no-man's-land in the heart of the fighting and, amazingly, was still operating on a limited basis. Despite damage to the

front of the building, the bank's vault was still one of the most secure in the region, housing many valuables.

After conducting one last check on equipment and the surrounding area, the men's commander signaled that it was time. Two men manned a 60mm mortar tube and began lobbing rounds into the distance to serve as a distraction. The rest of the team loaded grenades into their M203s, aimed at the building's windows and doors, and fired. Getting through the broken windows and doors, the thieves ran into the bank's lobby and ensured the first floor was clear.

Once the building was secured, the team changed their focus to getting into the vault. The vault door was several inches thick, made of solid steel, and full of advanced locking mechanisms. They could get past it, but it would take time. Fortunately for them, there was another way to bypass the door.

The team spent the next hour constructing shaped charges—highly specialized explosives that can direct the force of the blast into a small area, making the explosion more potent—and attached them to the wall on the side of the vault. Once the area was clear, the shaped charges were detonated, blowing a huge hole through the wall and the vault.

Once inside the vault, the thieves spent the next few days loading up three truckloads worth of loot including gold bullion, cash, stocks, bonds, and more worth an approximate £25 million (worth over $210 million today). When all was said and done, the crew had pulled off the largest bank heist in history.

KNOWN SUSPECTS

To this day, nobody has ever been charged in connection to this heist. While there are no official suspects, there are two predominant theories about who could have pulled off a heist like this in the middle of a war zone, and both are equally interesting and plausible.

The most accepted theory is that the heist was planned and executed by Yasser Arafat's Palestine Liberation Organization (PLO). At this point in the Lebanese civil war, the PLO was the region's most powerful fighting force, and they would have had the access to the weapons and explosives needed to perform almost every part of the heist except for getting into the actual vault. For that part of the heist, it is said that the PLO hired a team of primarily Catholic Corsican safecrackers to get into the vault, in exchange for one of the truckloads

of loot. Once their truckload was secured, the Corsicans headed home with their money in a chartered plane, while the PLO took their two truckloads to Switzerland, whose notoriously lax banking laws were even more permissive at the time.

The second theory, which is also fairly plausible, is that the heist was unofficially performed by a team of British Secret Air Service (SAS) commandos. Officially, the SAS was never in Beirut at the time, but clandestine operations are not unheard of. The SAS would also have had access to the necessary weapons and explosives and would be one of the few organizations trained in creating shaped charges. According to this theory, the bank was targeted by Britain because several well-known terror groups (including the PLO) supposedly kept financial documents in the vault's safe-deposit boxes. Once the documents were secured, the rest of the vault's contents were stolen to make the operation look like a heist. While this theory has never been confirmed, there are some former SAS commandos that have admitted to performing the job.

THE CASE TODAY

The total value of the heist has never been made public and will forever be known only to the thieves. While most estimates place the haul at approximately £25 million, it was likely much higher due to the secretive nature of safe-deposit boxes. None of the money or gold has been recovered, and there are officially no suspects in the case.

THE BANCO CENTRAL HEIST

Ensure your bank is insured.

AUGUST 6, 2005 ★ *FORTALEZA, BRAZIL*

DESCRIPTION

After several weeks of painstaking digging, on Saturday, August 6, 2005, the thieves were ready to finish the last meter of the tunnel. It would be the hardest stretch yet. Instead of tunneling through soft Brazilian soil, they'd be breaking through steel-reinforced concrete and into the vault of Brazil's Banco Central at Fortaleza.

They had been preparing for this moment for quite some time. Three months prior, they rented a commercial property two blocks from the bank and used the storefront as an operations center and began excavation of a tunnel that would eventually stretch over 250 feet and lead directly under the central bank's vault. The thieves created a fake landscaping company to operate out of the storefront, which allowed them to move vans full of dirt and excavation equipment without raising suspicion. The thieves even prepared real and artificial turf and plants for

sale to help solidify the landscaping business alibi, which they'd named "Grama Sintetica" (Synthetic Turf).

Over the next three months, the crew used GPS sensors and math to ensure they were headed in the right direction while fortifying the tunnel, which was at least twelve feet below the surface, with wooden support beams for added strength and plastic to prevent water damage. Even more impressively, the tunnel was equipped with its own lighting and air circulation systems, and a pulley system to help move buckets of dirt quickly. Altogether, it's estimated that the tunnel cost approximately $200,000 to build.

Finally, with the tunnel complete, it was time to break through the concrete into the vault. After a bit of smashing and using blowtorches to cut through the concrete's steel reinforcements, the thieves were in. Sitting in front of them was 3.5 tons of

nonsequential $50 real bills that were waiting to be sorted and evaluated to see which bills were still fit for circulation. In total, the stack of cash was approximately 165 million reals, worth $70 million.

The thieves moved carefully to avoid motion detectors and disabled alarms inside the vault. They loaded the cash into bins that were hooked up to the tunnel's pulley system. Once a bin was full, it was pulled through the tunnel into the landscaping office, emptied, and sent back to the vault. The crew worked tirelessly throughout the weekend, but by late Sunday evening they'd stolen all 165 million reals, approximately 3,300,000 individual $50 bills. They emptied most of their belongings from the office, covered everything in burned lime to conceal fingerprints, and disappeared.

The heist was discovered the following morning when bank employees opened the vault and saw that it was emptied. Unfortunately for the bank, they hadn't bothered to insure the money because they felt that the risk was too low and the premiums were too high.

KNOWN SUSPECTS

Police dusted the vault for fingerprints. While the vault was covered in burned lime, rendering most of the prints useless, they did manage to get at least one partial print at the crime scene. They followed the tunnel into the office building and discovered that the thieves had left behind little evidence besides bolt cutters, blowtorches, and an electric saw. Police also found a prepaid phone card in the tunnel.

Only a day later, police would catch a big break when a man tried to purchase ten cars with cash in an especially poor region of Brazil. Police managed to locate the truck hauling the cars and discovered bundles of cash in three of the cars worth a total of over 2 million reals. After arresting the man, police were able to get him to testify against his compatriots in exchange for immunity and anonymity.

The informant told police that they'd been helped by an inside man, who provided the location of the bank's motion detectors and alarm systems and informed the robbers that the security cameras worked in real time but did not actually record anything. The informant also told police that the tunnel had been partially financed by the mayor of nearby Boa Viagem, a small village to the south of Fortaleza.

The following month, five men were arrested with $5 million reals and told police that they'd been hired to help dig the tunnel along with eighteen other men. These five men were arrested after being caught trying to charter a jet out of Brazil.

One of the gang's suspected ringleaders, Marcio Pierre, was arrested over a year after the heist.

THE CASE TODAY

To date, over fifty suspects have been arrested in connection to the heist, the majority of whom were tied to the construction of the tunnel. Many of the arrests were connected to the prepaid phone card found in the tunnel, which helped police identify over forty phone numbers that had been called using the card.

It is likely that investigators will never truly know how many people were involved in this heist or be able to bring them to justice. Luis Fernando Ribeiro was identified as one of the gang's ringleaders, but before police could arrest him, he was kidnapped. After Ribeiro's family paid nearly a million reals for his ransom, the kidnappers executed Luis and dumped his body. Over the next year, six other members of the gang would be kidnapped for ransom due to the heist, and several more would be found murdered.

Of the suspects that have been arrested, twenty-six of them have been sentenced to prison for anywhere from three to eighty years. Several of the thieves have used their tunneling skills to break out of jail, including the chief engineer of the tunnel, nicknamed "Big Boss."

So far, police have only recovered approximately $20 million reals. Due to the fact that the bills were unmarked and nonsequential, it is highly unlikely that the rest of the money will ever be found.

A NOTORIOUS NE'ER-DO-WELL

The king of the bank robbers.

WHO: GEORGE LEONIDAS LESLIE
WHEN: 1842–1878
WHERE: NEW YORK, NEW YORK

If you've ever seen a heist movie, you've probably watched a scene where the thieves are poring over schematics or practicing their safecracking skills on a perfect replica of the Bellagio's vault. What you might not know, however, is that these clichés are all based on the real-life King of Bank Robbers, George Leonidas Leslie.

Leslie was born in 1842 and raised in Cincinnati, Ohio. The son of a wealthy brewery owner, he dreamed of becoming an architect and began taking coursework to help him meet that end. While in school, he was drafted to fight for the Union army in the US Civil War, but his father paid $300 to prevent him from going to war, which led to much local criticism. Eventually, Leslie graduated from the University of Cincinnati at the top of his class with a degree in architecture. After graduation, he started a successful architectural firm in Cincinnati, but his parents' death left him in charge of their brewery and his own firm. Leslie sold both businesses and moved to New York City.

After arriving in New York, Leslie quickly became caught up in the city's criminal underground and used his architectural knowledge to climb up the ranks. Leslie proved to be especially adept at bank robberies, particularly when it came to reconnaissance and planning, as he used his knowledge of architecture to determine the layouts of banks and even built detailed scale models to walk through with his team quickly and accurately. Due to his legitimate credentials in the world of architecture, Leslie would sometimes borrow the actual blueprints used to build banks that he was targeting. Other times, Leslie would go to a bank and rent a safe-deposit box so that he could go inside and observe its security measures. Or he'd get one of his gang members hired as a watchman so that they could relay that information to him.

Leslie even constructed full-scale models of the vaults for his team to practice in, complete with the exact vault doors and safes used by the bank to ensure that everything was as accurate as possible. When it came time to open the vault doors, Leslie invented an ingenious solution for that, too. By placing a small tin disk called the "Little Joker" behind a vault or safe dial in the weeks leading up to the heist, Leslie could retrieve the Little Joker and see the combination numbers imprinted in the tin. While this did require breaking into the bank to install the joker and then entering once again to retrieve it, this wasn't an issue for Leslie, who would sometimes break into a bank several times before a robbery just to make sure everything was ready.

Leslie didn't perform these heists alone, though. Over the years, he put together one of the most impressive gangs and crime networks of America's Gilded Age, including Thomas "Shang" Draper, Red Leary, and Fredericka "Marm" Mandelbaum, who was New York City's most notorious fence of the time. At their peak, Leslie and his gang were responsible for over 80 percent of the bank robberies in the United States. Due to Leslie's meticulous planning, the heists almost never involved violence.

Shortly before pulling off what would be the gang's biggest heist, Leslie made the mistake of having affairs with the wives of both Shang Draper and Red Leary. When Draper found out, he shot and killed Leslie and dumped his body at Tramp's Rock in Yonkers, New York, where it was found on June 4, 1878.

CHAPTER 3

IT BELONGS IN A MUSEUM!

For the refined thief, nothing inspires awe more than getting your hands on a painting by one of the masters. To know that Leonardo da Vinci was the first person to touch something and you were the last would feel like holding a piece of history. Well, holding it for ransom at least. Whether you're stealing the *Mona Lisa* or grabbing half a billion dollars' worth of art in Boston, these heists may take place in museums, but they belong in the Hall of Fame.

THE ISABELLA STEWART GARDNER MUSEUM HEIST

The biggest art heist in history.

MARCH 18, 1990 ★ *BOSTON, MASSACHUSETTS*

DESCRIPTION

The Isabella Stewart Gardner Museum was built at the direction of wealthy philanthropist and art collector Isabella Stewart Gardner, as a place to store and display her ever-growing personal art collection. Designed to look like a fifteenth-century Venetian palace, Isabella stocked the building with works by Vermeer, Rembrandt, Michelangelo, Raphael, Manet, and Degas, and hers was the first collection in North America to feature works by Botticelli. In addition to the paintings, Gardner also collected thousands of rare books and objects from all over the world and all across history. She opened the museum to the public in 1903 and continued to grow her collection until her death in 1924. As part of her will, Gardner stipulated that the museum should remain open and that the collection should never be rearranged or have pieces bought or sold.

In the early morning hours of Sunday, March 18, 1990, the city of Boston was in the throes of yet another wild St. Patrick's Day celebration. Bars were packed, the streets were filled with the sounds of partiers, and police were busy responding to various incidents all over town. Inside the museum, security guards Rick Abath and Randy Hestand noticed several fire alarms going off in various rooms, but closer inspection revealed that there was neither smoke nor fire anywhere in the building. Believing the alarm system to be malfunctioning, Abath turned off the security panel.

Approximately twenty minutes later, two police officers approached the side door of the museum and rang the buzzer. When Abath answered, the officers told him that they were responding to a disturbance call and needed to be buzzed in so they could investigate. Assuming that perhaps this was related to the false fire alarms, he buzzed them in at 1:24 a.m. The two police officers entered a locked foyer and approached Abath at the security desk. They asked if there were any other guards on patrol, and had Abath radio to Hestand to come back to the security desk.

One of the officers told Abath that he matched the profile of a suspect that had a warrant out for his arrest and asked him to present his ID so he could be ruled out. Abath did as he was told, moving away from the only alarm button at his desk. This officer pushed Abath against the wall and handcuffed him. Hestand entered the room shortly after and was handcuffed by the other officer. With both guards handcuffed, the officers removed their false mustaches, and told the guards that they were robbing them and that they needed to cooperate if they wanted to survive.

Next, the robbers duct-taped the guards' hands and heads and led them into the basement, where they handcuffed both of them to steam pipes. The thieves took the guards' wallets, told them that they had their addresses, and promised them a reward in a year if they cooperated. With the guards subdued, the men headed back upstairs to the museum.

Over the next seventy minutes, the thieves made their way through the museum and stole several pieces of artwork. Thanks to the museum's motion detectors, we know that the thieves first went into the Dutch Room on the second floor. They grabbed *Storm on the Sea of Galilee* and *A Lady and Gentleman in Black*, both by Rembrandt. The thieves smashed the frames on the ground to break the protective glass and then cut the paintings out of the wooden stretchers. Next, they stole a small self-portrait of Rembrandt, approximately the size of a postage stamp, and then Vermeer's *The Concert* and Flinck's *Landscape with Obelisk*. Finally, on their way to the next room, they took an ancient Chinese vase called a "gu."

Next the thieves went to a narrow hallway nicknamed "The Short Gallery" and stole five sketches by Degas and an eagle-shaped finial that sat atop a flagpole used by Napoleon. Finally, the thieves headed back downstairs and stole Manet's *Chez Tortoni*, which had been hanging in the Blue Room. After consolidating the stolen art, they went back down to the basement to ensure the guards were still tied to the pipes and asked if they were comfortable. Finally, they went up to the security desk and took the CCTV tapes and the motion-detector printouts, not knowing that the motion-detector data was also backed up on a separate hard drive. After making at least two trips to a red Dodge Daytona that was parked near the side door, the thieves left the museum.

In just eighty-one minutes, they had managed to steal close to half a billion dollars in art, making this case the largest art heist in American history.

KNOWN SUSPECTS

To this day, nobody has ever been arrested in connection with the Isabella Stewart Gardner heist, but police have had no shortage of credible suspects, from famed Boston gangster Whitey Bulger to the security guard, Rick Abath.

Abath was viewed as a strong suspect because of his knowledge of the museum's security systems and layout, and because he had been the person to shut down the alarms that night and buzz in the thieves. When police investigated the motion-detector logs, they discovered that the Blue Room had only detected motion when Abath was doing his rounds earlier in the night, making it likely that Abath had removed the Manet work before the thieves arrived. Ultimately, Abath was cleared as a suspect because investigators thought he was too incompetent to have aided in the robbery.

Another suspect was Boston con man Brian McDevitt, who had previously tried to rob an art gallery in Glens Falls, New York, called The Hyde Collection using a very similar MO. McDevitt had dressed as a FedEx driver and tried to handcuff a guard and steal a Rembrandt. McDevitt was also strangely interested in flags and loosely matched the description of the taller thief. McDevitt was cleared when his fingerprints were found not to match any of the ones at the crime scene.

Whitey Bulger was the king of Boston's criminal underworld at the time and so was a potential suspect in any crime that took place in the area. Investigators thought that his close ties with corrupt Boston police officers would have made it easy for him to get the police uniforms for the thieves, and his relationship with the IRA would have made it easy for him to move the paintings. Bulger proclaimed his innocence and stated that he also wanted to find the thieves because he wanted a tribute payment for pulling off such a large job on his home turf. No evidence linking Bulger or the IRA to the crime was ever found.

THE CASE TODAY

Unfortunately, this case has never been solved and remains open to this day. None of the art has ever been recovered. In keeping with Isabella Stewart Gardner's wishes, the stolen paintings have never been replaced, and their empty frames are displayed where the paintings once hung.

THE BOTCHED BANKSY JOB

This heist was off-the-wall crazy.

WHAT: BANKSY'S UMBRELLA GIRL
WHEN: FEBRUARY 2014
WHERE: NEW ORLEANS, LOUISIANA

In most art heists, crafty thieves quietly sneak into a museum after dark and carefully lift paintings off the wall before making their escape into the night. The next morning, when guards walk by an empty picture frame or bare wall, they do a panicked double take and sound the alarm. But what do you do when the painting is part of the wall?

After famed graffiti artist Banksy left one of his trademark stenciled murals, *Umbrella Girl*, on a building at 1034 North Rampart Street in New Orleans, two men decided that seeing it on the street was not enough; they needed to steal the painting. The only problem was that wherever the painting went, the brick wall needed to follow. In February 2014, the thieves decided to steal the painting, wall and all.

Just before 1:00 p.m., the men drove up to the painting in a white moving truck and parked. One of the thieves donned a Home Depot apron. After grabbing some tools, the men took a drill and began drilling holes into the wall in a rectangle around the painting. Once the holes were drilled, the thieves began using a chisel and hammer to try to remove the entire section of wall. Before long, two more men arrived to assist.

WHAT WENT WRONG

Unfortunately for them, what the thieves had in terms of work ethic, they lacked in common sense and timing. Neighbors and passersby could hear the drilling and chiseling and see the men attempting to steal an entire wall in broad daylight. One of the witnesses even took photos of them in the act and posted them to Facebook.

Neighbors approached the men and began questioning them about what they were doing. One of the thieves told the neighbors that they had been hired to remove the painting at the building owner's request so it could be placed in a museum, but when they were asked which museum the painting was headed to, the thieves were unable to answer or produce any kind of permit or paperwork. After realizing their cover was blown, the thieves gave up on the project at approximately 4:30 p.m. and drove off in the van empty-handed.

KNOWN SUSPECTS

In March 2014, one of the suspects in the attempted heist, Christopher Sensabaugh, was named by police. Sensabaugh, then a thirty-year-old Los Angeles resident, is believed to have been the man with the drill during the heist. Police have issued a warrant for his arrest but have not been able to apprehend him yet.

THE *MONA LISA* OF HEISTS

The heist that turned the *Mona Lisa* into a global phenomenon.

AUGUST 21, 1911 ★ *PARIS, FRANCE*

DESCRIPTION

Early in the morning of August 21, 1911, three men opened the door and walked out of the supply closet they'd spent the night in at the Louvre. They made their way down to the Salon Carre, and looked up at a familiar face, the *Mona Lisa*. The men lifted the painting, its frame, and protective glass case off the wall, and then removed the wooden canvas from the case and frame. Covering the painting with a blanket, the men ran out of the front door of the Louvre and boarded a 7:47 a.m. train at Quai d'Orsay with the masterpiece in hand.

Today, the *Mona Lisa* is probably the most famous painting on earth, but at the time of the theft, it was not a particularly well-known work outside of art circles. While da Vinci was certainly a celebrated and revered artist, the *Mona Lisa* was nowhere near as popular as *The Last Supper,* and, as a result, the theft wasn't even noticed until twenty-eight hours later, when a still-life artist noticed the bare hooks on the wall where the painting had been. Even then, he assumed that it might have been taken down for restoration work, or as part of the Louvre's efforts to photograph all of the museum's works. It wasn't until he asked a guard when the painting would be returned that the museum realized it had been stolen.

When word of the theft hit the news, the *Mona Lisa* quickly became the most famous painting in the world. France immediately dispatched over sixty detectives to search for it, hoping to bring the national scandal to a quick end. Suspicions ranged from banking magnate J. P. Morgan commissioning the theft to German nationals acting on the orders of Kaiser Wilhelm due to the increasingly strained relations between France and Germany in the era immediately prior to the First World War.

Still, every lead that the detectives chased went nowhere. After a week of frantic searching, the painting was no closer to being found and the Louvre was forced to reopen without the painting. Throngs of spectators came to see the empty frame, and newspapers ran nearly constant stories about the painting, offering increasingly larger rewards for the return of the masterpiece.

As the buzz around the theft grew, the thieves realized that they would not be able to sell the work as quickly as hoped and hid the wooden canvas in the false bottom of a steamer trunk.

KNOWN SUSPECTS

Two years after the theft, a man walked into an art dealer's office in Florence, Italy looking to sell a painting. The art dealer immediately recognized the painting, as Leonardo da Vinci was one of Florence's proudest sons, and the River Arno, which runs through Florence, was actually the background of the *Mona Lisa*. The dealer brought in the head of an Italian art gallery, and after inspecting the stamp on the back of the painting, they were able to confirm that this was in fact *Mona Lisa*. The art dealer told the man to come back later to get his money and took down his name and contact information.

Thirty minutes later, police arrived at the home of Vincenzo Perugia and arrested him for the theft. It was discovered that Perugia worked at the Louvre and was actually the person that built the glass display case for *Mona Lisa*. When he and his two accomplices—brothers named Vincenzo and Michele Lancelotti— stole the painting, Perugia used his knowledge of the case to get it opened quickly without damaging the work.

THE CASE TODAY

When questioned about his motive, Perugia claimed that he was acting in the interest of Italy by returning the painting to its ancestral home after Napoleon had stolen it for France decades earlier. Perugia was sentenced to eight months in prison; World War I officially started just days after the trial. While the war dominated headlines, the *Mona Lisa* never left the limelight and remains the most famous work of art in the world.

THE MEXICO CITY ANTHROPOLOGICAL MUSEUM HEIST

Why study history when you can steal it?

DECEMBER 25, 1985 ★ *MEXICO CITY, MEXICO*

DESCRIPTION

In the early morning hours of Christmas Day 1985, two thieves made their way to the grounds of the National Museum of Anthropology in Mexico City. After scaling the museum's fence, they made their way to an air conditioning vent. They opened a hole in the duct, crawled inside, and made their way into the museum.

Once inside, they made their way to a glass display case. After checking their notes, they carefully opened the case and extracted the most valuable items inside. Next, they moved to another case and stole several more artifacts, including a pre-Columbian jade mosaic face mask. Over the next thirty minutes, they would loot dozens of items from seven display cases. Once they'd grabbed everything they

came for, they went back to the vent, moving carefully to avoid triggering the museum's alarm systems.

Luckily for the thieves, the alarms had been malfunctioning since the devastating 8.0 earthquake that had hit Mexico City a few months prior. Luckier still was the fact that all nine of the security guards had been too busy drinking and celebrating at an impromptu Christmas party to monitor the cameras or perform their rounds.

After exiting through the same vent shaft, they jumped over the fence and into a car they'd parked nearby. They'd just pulled off a heist that wasn't just worth a billion dollars; it was priceless.

KNOWN SUSPECTS

News of the heist rocked the nation: 124 artifacts from the Aztec, Mayan, Mixtec, and Zapotec empire had been taken, and were considered to be national treasures. While police investigated, theories of who was responsible became a national obsession. Some thought the cartels were behind the heist, but most theorized that the thieves had been foreign, and many suggested the CIA or KGB were behind the heist. Wherever they were from, police were certain that this was the work of sophisticated pros.

What police didn't yet know was that this heist wasn't the work of foreign agents, or even professionals. This heist had been pulled off by two friends with no criminal records. They were, in fact, a pair of friends who dropped out of veterinary school together. Carlos Perches Trevino and Roman Sardina Garcia spent over six months planning the heist, including nearly daily visits to the museum to identify the most valuable items, and sketching the security alarm and camera locations. After they pulled it off, they stored the artifacts in a duffel bag in the back of a closet.

Trevino and Garcia waited over a year to do anything with the artifacts. After Trevino felt the coast was clear, he took the pieces to Acapulco. From there, Trevino was able to connect with a cartel drug trafficker named Salvador Gutierrez, and exchanged a few pieces for an unspecified amount of cocaine. While Trevino and Garcia began planning a deal to exchange the rest of the items, Gutierrez was arrested on trafficking charges. While being interrogated by police, he mentioned the artifacts and soon police investigated Garcia and Trevino.

THE CASE TODAY

On June 9, 1989, Trevino traveled back to Mexico City with the rest of the artifacts and was arrested by federal agents, who discovered 111 of the artifacts in his closet. His brother, Luis, was also arrested for covering up for Trevino. Garcia managed to evade authorities and remains on the run to this day. A few days after Trevino's arrest, the museum announced the recovery of the artifacts. They commemorated the occasion with a brand-new exhibition featuring the stolen items and their contributions to culture. The exhibition was a massive success, and the museum saw a marked increase in attendance for years after the heist.

Trevino was tried for charges that included "theft and damage to national treasures," which carried a sentence of ten years in prison. He was also charged with various drug and trafficking charges, which carried a maximum sentence of twenty-five years. After a lengthy trial in 1992, Trevino was sentenced to twenty-two years total, but was released on probation in 1995. All but the seven artifacts Garcia stole have been recovered.

TOOLS OF THE TRADE: THE LOCKPICK

No key? No problem.

WHAT IS IT?

Invented in the 1770s, a lockpick is a stealthy burglar's best friend, and one of the quintessential thief tools. Typically, lockpick sets consist of two main parts: a torsion bar and the pick itself. When used by a skilled burglar, a lockpick can open doors within a few seconds—sometimes less if the burglar is using an electric lockpick or a lockpick gun. Although lockpicks will not work for every type of lock, they can be reliably used almost anywhere a key is used.

Lockpicks come in many shapes, including simple hooks, snowmen patterns, and wavy lines. Each pick shape has advantages and disadvantages, but in the hands of a skilled picker, any shape can be used effectively. Typically, choosing a lockpick comes down to personal preference.

HOW DOES IT WORK?

Lockpicks work by lining up the pins in a lock with the shear line in the lock's cylinder. If the pins are lined up properly, the cylinder can turn and the lock opens, but if even one pin is too far above or below the line, it blocks the cylinder from being able to rotate and the lock remains closed.

The torsion bar puts steady light pressure on the cylinder so that it will start to turn as soon as the pins are properly lined up. With the torsion bar in use, the lockpick can be inserted into the lock to begin moving the pins into position. As each pin is placed into position, the tension from the torsion bar helps to keep it in place until the cylinder is able to rotate. While some thieves move from pin to pin individually, many use lockpick guns or electric lockpicks to jostle the pins even faster than by hand.

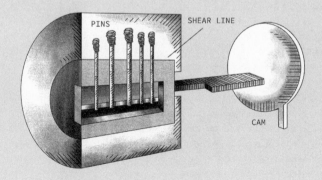

PINS

SHEAR LINE

CAM

THE QUEEN'S WATCH

The world's most sophisticated watch was guarded by the world's least sophisticated security system.

APRIL 15, 1983 ★ *JERUSALEM, ISRAEL*

DESCRIPTION

On the evening of April 15, 1983, a sedan drove through the streets of Jerusalem toward the L. A. Mayer Museum for Islamic Art. The three-story building boasted an incredible collection of art from the Muslim world that spanned centuries and was home to one of the world's finest watch collections, including what was perhaps the most expensive and beautiful watch in the history of the world.

The pocket watch, known as The Queen, was a stunning work of crafts-manship and art, hand-built by Swiss master horologist Abraham-Louis Breguet for French queen Marie Antoinette. Breguet was instructed to spare no detail or expense in making the watch, which was adorned in gold and diamonds; sapphires were used to reduce friction. The watch is a marvel of engineering, featuring a skipping hour hand, full perpetual calendar,

a device that chimed the time on the hour, and, incredibly, a thermometer. It consisted of over 820 individual parts and featured twenty-three complications (horological speak for any feature that goes beyond displaying hours, minutes, or seconds). The watch was so complex that it took Breguet forty-four years to complete it, by which time Marie Antoinette had been dead for thirty-four years.

Back in Jerusalem, the driver pulled up close to the museum and parked the car. He exited the vehicle and removed a small hydraulic tire jack from the trunk. He moved to the iron fence protecting the building and placed the jack sideways between two of the fence's bars. After a few minutes of using the jack, the bars were spread apart far enough for him to slink through to the building, where he approached a window and installed a rope ladder using a set of hooks. Once he'd climbed approximately ten feet up, he pried open a window using a screwdriver and entered the museum.

Over the next several hours, the thief took advantage of the museum's faulty security system and plundered several works of art before heading to the back of the museum where the watches were on display. Astonishingly, the display case for the watches was not even attached to the security system. The burglar took just over half of the watches on display, including The Queen, and then headed back to his car, needing several trips to move all of his loot. When the car was loaded, he drove off and disappeared into the Jerusalem traffic.

Authorities and museum officials were stunned by the theft. They'd had the watch collection insured for $700,000, but the many of the watches were worth more than that by themselves. The Queen alone was reportedly valued at over $30 million. Investigators hired former Mossad operatives to assist in the investigation, but the thief had left them next to nothing in the way of physical evidence, and even less in the way of witnesses.

KNOWN SUSPECTS

With the investigation going nowhere quickly, police began checking auctions and marketplaces to see if any of the watches appeared. If credible tips came in, authorities would travel to Europe or Asia to investigate, but over the span of twenty-three years, not a single lead panned out. Finally, in 2006, the L. A. Mayer Museum was contacted by a lawyer seeking to sell back the artifacts on behalf of an anonymous seller. The museum contacted authorities, who quickly identified the seller as an American high school teacher named Nili Shamrat. Shamrat was brought into custody and told police that her husband, a well-known Israeli thief named Na'aman Diller, had made a deathbed confession to her about having pulled off the heist. Diller revealed that he'd kept the artifacts and watches in storage in Tel Aviv, and when police searched the storage unit, they discovered all of the pieces tucked away in boxes, wrapped in newspaper. Diller had taken meticulous notes of how each of the watches worked, how to maintain them, and how and when to wind and oil them.

Diller was something of a legend in the Israeli criminal underground. Renowned for his ability to crawl into tight spaces, his skills as a master forger and resourceful thief made him known around the world for his abilities. This was particularly true after a 1967 bank robbery in Tel Aviv, in which he spent five months tunneling into the vault using an elaborate oxygen delivery system.

When the L. A. Mayer museum was robbed, Diller was initially considered a suspect, but he was able to provide forged travel documents that placed him out of the country during the heist. His alibi was solid enough for him to be removed from the suspect list.

THE CASE TODAY

While there was initially suspicion around Shamrat's desire to sell the pieces back to the museum, investigators eventually determined that she had not committed any crimes, and did not pursue charges, though she was fired from her teaching job due to the case. The artifacts and watches were returned to the L. A. Mayer museum, where they remain on display to this day—this time with a working alarm system.

THE TRING FEATHER HEIST

This heist is for the birds.

NOVEMBER 12, 2010 ★ *TRING, UNITED KINGDOM*

DESCRIPTION

The Natural History Museum at Tring is an unsuspecting Tudor-style building approximately an hour outside of London's city center. Originally the private museum of the Second Baron Rothschild, Lionel Walter, the museum is home to one of the world's most pristine collections of taxidermic animals, including a staggering collection of bird skins collected by famed naturalist Alfred Russel Wallace.

Wallace was credited with independently finalizing his theory of evolution and natural selection at the same time as Charles Darwin while studying birds of paradise in Asia. He collected hundreds of thousands of specimens of birds, insects, reptiles, and mammals throughout his journeys, which are still used for scientific study to this day.

Originally, the specimens were housed in London, but during the Blitz in World War II, the collection was moved out of the city to prevent it from being destroyed by bombing. The museum at Tring was selected to house the collection, and put thousands of animals on display, while keeping the other specimens, many still bearing the collection tags filled out by Wallace himself, preserved in an enormous series of cabinets and files in the museum's storage areas, where they are occasionally studied by researchers. The museum boasts one of the largest collections of extinct and endangered bird skins in the world. And it was taken completely by surprise when a light-fingered thief absconded with a suitcase crammed with millions of dollars' worth of bird skins.

KNOWN SUSPECTS

Although bird skins might seem like a strange thing to steal when compared to diamonds or cash, to the right buyer, these brightly colored feathers were worth their weight in gold. Fortunately for a twenty-year-old American flutist named Edwin Rist, he knew just the people that pay top dollar for the feathers: salmon fly tyers.

Rist was something of a prodigy in the world of fly-tying. As an adolescent, he took a few lessons tying trout fishing lures, loving how he was able to make a hook and feathers and string mimic an insect. Before long, he was obsessed with the craft and started looking into the considerably more vibrant and complex salmon flies. Designs for some salmon flies dated back over a century, and the "recipes" required the feathers of birds from all over the world. Because of the rarity of the feathers many of the designs required, tyers often learned to create substitutes or dyed more readily available feathers to fit the bill.

Rist quickly became known in fly-tying circles. First, he stood out for his age, but before long, it was his talent alone that made him stand out. Still, Rist knew that he would never truly be able to make a name for himself in the sport until he could make his flies using the original Victorian recipes. He bought what feathers he could find online, amazed to see the prices that could be paid for a single feather from an endangered or extinct species. He began working on increasingly elite flies, but always looked for ways to get his hands on any feathers that were rarer still.

Through a stroke of good fortune, Rist was selected to attend the British Royal Academy of Music in London. Rist was an accomplished flutist and planned to use this time to focus on his dream of playing in the Berlin Symphony Orchestra instead of fly-tying, but when he heard about the museum's collection of rare birds, he had to go see for himself. Using his real name but false pretenses, Rist pretended to be a graduate student working on a project involving the birds and was given a tour of the facility. Rist was blown away by the collection and was even able to photograph and catalog where each type of specimen was kept within the giant file cabinets.

After seeing so many of these exotic feathers, Rist knew he had to steal them. He made notes of the facility's security and then headed back to London.

After a performance on the night of November 12, 2010, Rist exited the Midland train and walked from the station to the Tring museum, wheeling a carry-on suitcase behind him. After dipping into an alley behind the museum, he pulled wire cutters out of his bag and removed the triple-stranded barbed wire on top of the security fence. Once the fence was clear, he climbed the seven-foot wall with his suitcase and pulled out a diamond-blade glass cutter. Leaning over from atop the wall, he traced the glass cutter on the window.

Suddenly, he fumbled the cutter and it dropped to the ground in an unreachable space between the building and the wall. Rist looked around and found a rock to smash the window. Once the glass was broken, he used the suitcase to push out the glass and entered into the museum's hallway, setting off a silent alarm in the process. After orienting himself, he took off in a fast walk toward the vault, moving all the quicker because he'd been given a tour of the museum and still had the layout fresh in his mind.

After a few minutes, he was in the vault room, an enormous space filled with hundreds of large white steel filing cabinets. Remembering where the most desirable birds were from his previous trip, he went to the first cabinet and began emptying dozens of bird specimens into his suitcase. First, a dozen fruit crows. Next, nearly forty resplendent quetzals, each of them nearly four feet long.

Rist moved from row to row, stuffing his suitcase with hundreds of rare bird skins, each species of bird more brightly plumed than the last. After realizing that he had no idea how long he'd been inside, Rist zipped up his suitcase and headed back to the same window he'd entered, hoping that the security guard hadn't noticed the broken glass while doing his rounds. Luckily for Rist, the security guard had been too busy watching a soccer game to notice that the alarm had gone off, or to perform his rounds. By the time the guard began patrolling the building, Rist had already climbed out the window and headed back to the train station, where he boarded a 3:54 a.m. train back to London with a suitcase full of 299 bird skins worth millions of dollars.

THE CASE TODAY

Almost immediately after the heist, Rist began selling the feathers in various online fly-tying message boards, and often on eBay using the name "Fluteplayer 1988." Rist sold lone feathers all the way up to entire skins, sometimes for thousands of dollars apiece. The influx of museum-quality feathers turned heads in fly-tying circles, and it didn't take long for some of the buyers to spot the connection between these birds and the robbery at Tring, which had made headlines all over the world.

Just over a year after the heist, a few members of the fly-tying community suggested that police look into Rist. He was arrested on the morning of November 12, 2010, at his apartment near the Royal Academy. Knowing he had been caught red-handed, Rist confessed in the hopes of getting a lighter sentence. Though he'd managed to sell at least 130 of the skins already, authorities were able to recover the remaining specimens from his apartment and later found incriminating evidence on his computer, like a Word doc detailing the heist called "PLAN FOR MUSEUM INVASION."

Rist also provided the names of his primary buyers of the black-market birds, as well as lists of what they'd purchased. Following his cooperation, Rist was given a suspended sentence of twelve months in prison, and twelve months of supervision, and he was ordered to pay restitution for any money he'd made selling the feathers, at least $125,000. But he didn't spend a single night in jail. Following his sentence, Rist graduated from the Royal Academy and is currently living his dream of playing the flute in the Berlin Symphony Orchestra under an assumed name.

THE TRANSYLVANIA BOOK HEIST

These thieves were more street-smart than book smart.

DECEMBER 17, 2004 ★ *LEXINGTON, KENTUCKY*

DESCRIPTION

On the morning of December 17, 2004, Transylvania University librarian Betty Jean Gooch—known affectionately to her students and colleagues as "BJ"—prepared the special collections room of the library for an upcoming appointment. She'd been emailed earlier by a man calling himself Walter Beckman, asking for a viewing of some of the library's most prized books, including a first-edition copy of Charles Darwin's *On the Origins of Species* and John James Audubon's *Birds of America*. The latter consisted of four double-sized volumes measuring over two-and-a-half feet wide, full of immaculately detailed paintings by Audubon himself, and was worth an estimated $10–$12 million. The full set of *Birds of America* weighed approximately 250 pounds.

Just before 11:00 a.m., Beckman entered the library and signed in for his appointment. Beckman asked Gooch if one of his friends could join

him for the viewing. Gooch agreed, and a few minutes later another man, calling himself John, entered the library. He and Beckman were dressed similarly, both wearing large overcoats, backpacks, hats, and gloves. Gooch led the men into the library's Rare Book Room, and one of the men closed the door behind them. Moments later, Beckman used a stun gun on Gooch, and she collapsed. Both men used zip ties to bind Gooch's hands and feet, pulled one of their hats over her eyes, and made their way to the display cases. One of the men urged her to stay down, saying, "Quit struggling, BJ, or do you want to feel more pain?"

Next, the thieves laid a bedsheet on the floor and began stacking the full set of Audubon books on the sheet and filling their backpacks with more manageable-sized books. The folios proved to be much heavier than they anticipated, and they only managed to carry three of the volumes out of the room. The thieves went to an employee-only elevator but got out on the wrong floor and were unable to find an exit, drawing the attention of a second librarian. While the thieves had planned on only one librarian working that day, the school's final-exam schedule meant that the library was full of both staff and students. They went back to the elevator, took it to the ground floor, and carried the books in the sheet to a stairwell that they hoped led to an exit.

As they were in the stairwell, the librarian that had spotted them earlier discovered Gooch still tied up on the floor of the Rare Book Room and chased the thieves. The two men dropped the Audubon books and ran out of the building to their getaway car with the librarian close behind. Once inside the minivan, the driver hurried down Fourth Street.

While they hadn't been able to take the Audubon books, their backpacks still contained rare books worth approximately $750,000, including the first-edition Darwin; a two-volume set of Hortus Sanitatis, worth approximately $450,000; and several paintings and sketches by Audubon.

Once the thieves were about a mile away from campus, the driver panicked and kicked the men out of the minivan, promising to come back shortly with a new car to avoid suspicion. The two exited the van and continued walking away from the campus, which by now was full of police cars. After a few blocks, the thieves were chased again, this time by muggers who planned on stealing their wallets and bags. They ran several blocks and, by a stroke of luck, came across their getaway driver, who had just secured a new car, and they sped off.

KNOWN SUSPECTS

While the heist had not gone perfectly, it had been planned for several months by a group of college students led by Spencer Reinhard. Spencer, a talented art student, had first conceived of the heist while on a tour of the library as a prospective college student. When he saw that millions of dollars in books were protected only by a lone middle-aged

woman, he fantasized about the ways that money could change his life. Spencer jokingly mentioned the idea of the heist to his childhood best friend, Warren Lipka, and the two began their initial reconnaissance of the campus and the library. They documented what times the building was opened, the schedules of the librarians and other staff, and what

kind of security measures were in place.

When the two friends were not conducting recon, they were watching heist movies like *Ocean's Eleven* or *The Thomas Crown Affair*, looking for inspiration for their own caper. Warren looked for a way to sell the books, opting to have a buyer lined up before committing the theft. One of his friends put him in contact with a potential fence, who handed Warren an email address on a piece of paper in a clandestine meeting in New York's Central Park. Warren contacted the email address and arranged a meeting with a potential buyer in Amsterdam. Amazingly, the buyer said that they would be interested in purchasing the books, but only on the condition that they were appraised by a reputable auction house.

Warren created a fake email address again using the name Walter Beckman, and contacted appraisers at Christie's Auction House in New York City to set up a meeting. Warren and Reinhold continued to plan, but soon realized they needed help. They recruited Warren's friend, Eric Borsuk, and Charles "Chas" Allen II, who would serve as the getaway driver during the heist. With the crew at full strength, they finalized their plans. Warren would set up a meeting with the librarian using his assumed name and incapacitate her with a stun gun, while Eric came in moments later to help steal the books. Spencer would serve as a lookout, and Chas promised to secure a fast car that would be waiting outside the library to help them make their escape.

They agreed to perform the heist the week before winter break and planned a trip to New York to meet with the Christie's representatives immediately after. They told their parents that they'd planned a ski trip in West Virginia to explain their absence. In an effort to conceal their identities, they donned makeup and costumes to look like old men, but when they arrived at the library, the poor quality of the costumes caused everybody to stare at them and the thieves opted to try again the next day without the costumes.

THE CASE TODAY

The weekend after the heist, the four friends drove twelve hours to NYC for their appointment with Christie's. Warren dressed himself in a blue suit and red tie, while Spencer opted for his grandfather's vintage yellow blazer and a gold scarf, and the two went to their meeting while Chas and Eric waited around the corner in an SUV with the books. Warren and Spencer bumbled through the meeting, claiming to be the sole representatives of Walter Beckman, who they claimed was a wealthy man from Boston who had just inherited the books, but could not provide any further provenance. They went back to the car to get the books, which they kept in a wheeled suitcase. The books were wrapped in bedsheets and pillowcases, and after the Christie's rep inspected them, she asked for Spencer's cell phone number and informed the men that they would be in touch for next steps, though she recommended to her team that the auction house not pursue any further involvement.

The police took several weeks to investigate the case, but eventually they caught a break when they identified the email address Spencer had used to contact BJ Gooch to arrange their meeting at the time of the heist. After obtaining email records from Yahoo, police were able to find another outgoing email from the same account to set up a meeting with Christie's. FBI agents inter-viewed the appraiser from Christie's, who managed to provide them with physical descriptions of Spencer and Warren, as well as the phone number that she'd been given, which they were able to trace back to Spencer's father.

When police looked into Spencer's family, they found a photo of Spencer and Warren playing soccer on the front page of their local paper and were able to confirm the identities of both as the men who had gone into Christie's. They began following and monitoring the two and quickly learned the identities of Chas and Eric as well. Finally, on February 11, 2005, SWAT teams led coordinated strikes on the bungalow where Eric, Chas, and Warren lived and at Spencer's dorm room. All four men were arrested without incident, though Chas initially thought the raid was a robbery and nearly pulled a gun on the agents until he realized what was happening. Police found all of the books unharmed in a duffel bag.

All four men pled guilty to charges including theft of cultural artifacts from a public museum and interstate transportation of stolen property. They were sentenced to seven years in prison. The crime has since been turned into a feature film, *American Animals,* and each of the four thieves served as consultants and provided interviews for the film.

THE RUSSBOROUGH HOUSE HEIST

Ireland's most famous heist.

MAY 1, 1986 ★ *COUNTY WICKLOW, IRELAND*

DESCRIPTION

In the early hours of May 1, 1986, just after 2:00 a.m., a team of thieves moved through the woods surrounding Ireland's longest house, Russborough House. Built in 1755, the house was purchased by one of the heirs of the De Beers mining family and used to house and display his considerable art collection, which contained works by Goya, Gainsborough, and the collection's most famous work, Vermeer's *Lady Writing a Letter with Her Maid*.

Moving under the cover of darkness, the group of ten thieves tied white plastic bags to large sticks. Once a bag was tied on, the stick was placed into the ground, marking the trail back from the house to their getaway cars. When the thieves reached the building, they approached a large gallery window, and the group's leader put tape on one of the windowpanes. Once the window was properly taped, they broke the windowpane, and several of the thieves scrambled inside, setting off the museum's motion detectors and alarm systems.

While inside, the thieves used tape to cover up the room's motion sensors and left through the same window they'd used to enter, ensuring that a large heavy curtain concealed the broken pane before the museum's caretaker arrived to investigate. With the moonlight catching the plastic bags they'd tied to sticks, the thieves were able to make it back to their hiding spot in the wood line, where they waited for police to respond to the alarm. Minutes later, the police arrived and performed a quick walk-through with the caretaker. After seeing that nothing was missing, the police determined that it had been a false alarm and left Russborough House, while the hidden thieves watched.

An hour later, the thieves were sure that the police were gone and

that the caretaker had gone back to sleep, so they made their way back to the building and used the broken windowpane to reenter the museum. With the motion detectors covered in tape, they were free to move around the room and begin taking paintings. In the span of just six minutes, they stole eighteen paintings, including works by Goya and the Vermeer. In total, the paintings were worth over $45 million at the time of the theft ($106 million today).

Unfortunately for the thieves, the paintings' fame meant that they were incredibly difficult to sell. The thieves actually abandoned seven of the paintings on the side of the road on the night of the heist, and then drove into the wooded mountains surrounding Dublin and buried the rest of the works, waiting for a better time to try to sell the paintings. Meanwhile, every day the works were missing was more embarrassing for the police, much to the thieves' delight.

KNOWN SUSPECTS

Embarrassing the police was not the point of the heist, but it was certainly an added bonus for Martin Cahill. Cahill, affectionately known throughout Ireland as "The General," was the country's most notorious criminal and was responsible for crimes that ranged from multimillion dollar heists to extortion of hot dog vendors on Grafton Street. His feuds with police were the stuff of legend, and he was known to send out some of his crew to destroy the putting greens at the country clubs police officers frequented.

On another occasion, after noticing that the police had been trailing him and his associates for several weeks, Cahill had his men slash the tires of over 190 police cars. He then returned home to see that his own Mercedes-Benz had been smashed by police. Often, when Cahill knew he was being followed by law enforcement, he'd take long slow drives into the middle of the Irish countryside, knowing that police would need to keep up with him. Cahill would drive until both cars were nearly out of fuel and then would pull over, fill up his car with a gas can he'd kept in the trunk, and then leave the police car stranded without fuel in the middle of nowhere.

Desperate for a chance to finally bring Cahill to justice, Irish police reached out to their Dutch colleagues and arranged a multinational sting operation in 1987. Using a Dutch criminal to pose as a buyer for the works, the taskforce arranged a meeting between Cahill's gang and the buyer at Killakee woods.

At the meeting, the buyer was shown the paintings while police watched nearby, but a random low-flying plane spooked Cahill's gang and they packed up the paintings and fled. While police tried to close in on them, their radios failed and the thieves were able to slip away before being apprehended.

THE CASE TODAY

Following the failed sting, the paint-ings would not resurface again until 1990, when a Metsu was recovered in Turkey. Two years later, one of the stolen Gainsboroughs was found in London and two more appeared in London the following year. In September 1993, a major art bust took place at the Antwerp airport and four more of the Russborough House works were recovered, including the Vermeer and a Goya.

On August 18, 1994, Cahill left a house he was staying at and started driving into Ranelagh to return a rented copy of *Delta Force 3*. As he stopped at the corner of Oxford Road and Charleston Road, a man on a motorbike pulled next to his car and fired several rounds from a .357 Magnum. Cahill was hit in the chest and head by several bullets and died instantly. While nobody has been charged in his murder, it is speculated that Cahill was murdered by the IRA for selling some of the Russborough House paintings to the rival Ulster Volunteer Force (UVF), so they could sell them for weapons. Cahill's funeral was widely attended by Irish police who wanted to confirm that their longtime foe was actually dead.

All but two of the paintings from Russborough House have been recovered, and it is likely that the last two paintings are still buried in the hills surrounding Dublin, but Cahill died before he was able to reveal where they are hidden.

THE DUCHESS OF DEVONSHIRE HEIST

Great thieves stand on the shoulders of giants.

MAY 25, 1876 ★ _CLONDON, UNITED KINGDOM_

DESCRIPTION

On May 6, 1876, Thomas Gainsborough's portrait of Georgiana, Duchess of Devonshire sat in the gallery of London art dealer William Agnew. Agnew had shocked the world two days earlier when he purchased the work at an auction for $51,540, the highest price ever paid for a painting at auction at the time. Within days, throngs of people visited the gallery to look at the masterpiece. Most were content just to admire the work, but some had other plans, most notably Junius Spencer Morgan, who intended to purchase the work for his son, famed financier J. P. Morgan.

Unfortunately for J. P. Morgan, another admirer of the painting wanted it too. Just after midnight on May 25, 1876, a man and his gigantic bodyguard walked down Bond Street toward the Agnew gallery. When they

arrived at the building, the smaller man climbed onto his bodyguard's shoulders and opened a second-story window. Once the window was open, the man quietly pulled himself into the gallery and made his way to where The Duchess was on display. The thief pulled out a small but sharp knife and carefully cut the canvas out of the wooden stretcher and frame.

After removing the painting, the burglar carefully rolled the canvas paint side facing outward, and made his way back to the window. Using his giant bodyguard as a ladder once again, he climbed back down to the street and the pair walked off into the night.

KNOWN SUSPECTS

When the theft was discovered, news outlets went into an absolute frenzy. The story dominated headlines across the world, and reports of sightings of the painting would appear in newspapers for years after the crime. While many claimed to see the painting, hoping to earn a reward, in reality the Duchess was hidden away by one of the world's most notorious thieves: Adam Worth.

Worth had originally stolen the painting to use as a bargaining chip to get his brother, Joe, out of prison, but that proved unnecessary when Joe was released due to procedural errors during his trial. Due to the painting's notoriety, Worth could not sell the work, so he held onto the painting for over twenty-five years, usually traveling with it stored in the false bottom of a steamer trunk. Eventually, he sent it back home to his native United States where it remained in secure storage.

THE CASE TODAY

When Worth refused to pay his enormous bodyguard, Junka Phillips, for his role in the crime, Phillips reported Worth to Scotland Yard, but they were unable to find enough evidence to conclusively link him to

the crime. When Phillips tried to get Worth to discuss the heist with him while undercover police were around, Worth refused and promptly fired Phillip before leaving London for South Africa, where he stole half a million dollars in uncut diamonds.

In 1892, Worth was finally arrested for an unrelated crime in Belgium and sentenced to seven years in prison, during which time he was beaten by rival inmates and he received word that his wife had been committed to a psychiatric ward due to a mental breakdown. After five years, Worth was released for good behavior and he returned home to the United States to see his wife, who barely recognized him. Next, Worth traveled to New York City to see his children before arranging a meeting with William Pinkerton, who led the Pinkerton Detective Agency that had been investigating Worth for the past several years.

Worth struck a deal for the return of the Duchess to the Agnew gallery in exchange for $25,000, with Pinkerton acting as the deal's broker. Once the painting was returned to Agnew, it was almost immediately purchased by J. P. Morgan for $150,000.

A NOTORIOUS NE'ER-DO-WELL

The villain who inspired Dr. Moriarty.

WHO: ADAM WORTH, THE NAPOLEON OF CRIME
WHEN: 1844–1902
WHERE: ALL OVER THE WORLD

While many criminals consider themselves to be masterminds, few deserve the title more than Adam Worth. Worth was born in Germany in 1844 and moved to the United States with his family at the age of five. He joined the Union army at the age of seventeen and was injured in the second battle of Bull Run. When Worth learned that he was presumed dead, he left the hospital and began a life of crime. He moved to New York City and learned how to pickpocket.

Worth soon formed his own gang of pickpockets and quickly graduated to performing robberies and heists. He began working with the legendary fence Marm Mandelbaum, robbing banks for her and assisting when she needed friends broken out of jail. After discovering that the Pinkerton Detective Agency was on his tail for a heist in Boston, Worth fled to London and immediately began assembling several more crews of his own, getting entwined into the upper crust of London's criminal society.

Worth's short stature earned him the nickname "The Napoleon of Crime," but soon the title applied more to his brilliant mind than his size. Worth traveled the world in his 105-foot steam yacht, owned stables of racehorses, and founded his own diamond exchange that allowed him to sell his stolen diamonds for lower prices than the competition.

KNOWN HEISTS

Due to Worth's innate ability to commit crimes without leaving behind evidence, it is impossible to know exactly how many heists he pulled off, though he is credited with having stolen the most valuable painting in the world at the time, and pulling off one of Africa's largest diamond heists. While most of Adam Worth's crimes are unknown, his duality as a master thief and member of high society inspired Arthur Conan Doyle to create Sherlock Holmes' nemesis, Dr. James Moriarty.

CHAPTER 4
RUN THE JEWELS

Diamonds may be a girl's best friend, but they are also a thief's best friend. How else are you going to fit half a billion dollars in your pants pocket? As long as there have been precious jewels, there have been people trying to steal them in the craziest ways imaginable. In this chapter, we'll dive deep into some of history's most brazen and valuable heists, and some of the world's most notorious gangs of jewel thieves. From sports fans to senior citizens, nobody can resist that twinkle, and that's why diamonds are forever.

THE SUPER BOWL RING HEIST

Great thief. Terrible boyfriend.

JUNE 7, 2008 ★ *BOSTON, MASSACHUSETTS*

DESCRIPTION

At approximately 4:00 p.m., a rented white box truck parked in a lot near the E. A. Dion jewelry workshop. Inside the truck, three thieves were watching the building, occasionally taking sips from water bottles and smoking weed. The men were all dressed identically: black coveralls, rubber overboots, and gloves. Their coveralls had two breast pockets where they kept police scanners and radios, each with its own earpiece so the thieves could communicate and be tipped off to any police activity.

The thieves made a last-minute inspection of their tools and wiped everything down with Simple Green, an industrial cleaner, to remove any fingerprints. As night fell, two of the thieves, now wearing black balaclavas and headlamps, climbed to the one-story building's roof. The lead thief found an outlet on the roof and plugged in a portable cell phone jammer to disable any wireless alarm systems. He pulled out a burner phone and saw his five bars of service drop down to zero. With cell phone signals properly jammed, he cut the building's phone lines to disable wired phones as well.

With the building's alarm systems completely disabled, the thieves left the roof and waited in a nearby wood line for forty-five minutes to ensure that there wasn't an unknown alarm that had been triggered. When the thieves were confident that police would not be on their way, they climbed back onto the roof and began cutting a hole in the roof. Noise wasn't really an issue at this building, as it was located in an industrial park with a nearby highway providing constant ambient sound. The building's location was actually one of the reasons the thieves picked this target; the other, of course, was what was inside.

E. A. Dion, a Boston-area jeweler, had been chosen to create the Super Bowl rings for the New York Giants that year, after a last-minute Eli Manning touchdown won the game and ended New England's run at a perfect season. Between players, coaching staff, and team employees, approximately 150 official Super Bowl rings would be made, with several more custom-made replica rings made for the NFL's sponsors like RadioShack. Each ring would require well over a carat of diamonds and other precious stones, plus enough gold and silver to cast rings large enough to fit on an offensive lineman's finger. In addition to the Super Bowl rings, E. A. Dion had a large collection of traditional jewelry, gold, wedding bands, and antique coins. It was a literal treasure trove.

When the hole in the roof was completed, the two thieves dropped into the building. The other thief, known as the "peek," stood watch outside and had his radio ready to alert the inside team if any trouble arose. Inside, the two thieves moved around the building and propped open all of the building's doors to make it easier to move from room to room with their tools and any loot they might find. Using two fifty-five-gallon garbage cans, they moved carefully through each room, putting anything that might be valuable into the cans, including multiple five-pound bags

of gold and silver beads, and stacks of gold plates and ingots from the workroom weighing between thirty and forty pounds.

In the next room, they dumped rare coins into the trash cans, followed by wedding bands, necklaces, and bracelets. With the other rooms cleared out, it was time to go to the office where the building's six-foot-tall safe was located. Amazingly, at least fifty of the Super Bowl rings were just sitting out in the open in the office. The thieves dumped the rings into the garbage cans and worked on the safe, trying to drill several points to no avail. Finally, they decided to take the safe with them, using a nearby pallet jack to wheel it to the box truck and using a portable ramp to get it loaded on the truck. Next, the thieves loaded the two garbage cans into the truck, and then went back through the building to clean up. Finally, just before sunrise, they headed back up to the roof to collect the cell phone jammer, got into the truck, and drove back to their home base, a warehouse in Lynn, Massachusetts.

Once at the warehouse, the thieves changed out of their coveralls and began splitting up the loot. The two men who went inside the building took 50 percent and 40 percent respectively, while the lookout took the remaining share.

KNOWN SUSPECTS

Only a few hours after the burglary, an employee arrived to open the shop for the day, noticed the break-in, and called police immediately. When detectives arrived at the scene, they realized that this heist had been done by a highly proficient crew, who had taken almost anything that wasn't bolted down with them, including the pallet jack. The thieves had

been a little sloppy, though, and left behind some boot prints, an extension cord for the phone jammer, and a Milwaukee brand electromagnetic drill press that used a zip tie to keep the chuck key in place.

After interviewing E. A. Dion employees and ruling out an inside job, the detectives had a suspect in mind, a career criminal and talented thief named Sean Murphy. Murphy was an infamous figure in the greater Boston underworld and had a reputation as a highly skilled burglar who used his skills to rise to the top of a group of thieves known as the "Lynn Breakers." Murphy was no stranger to using fancy gadgets to rob anything from banks to pharmacies, and, on top of it all, he was a huge Patriots fan.

Still, there wasn't any conclusive evidence left behind at the scene to tie Murphy to the theft. So far, the biggest break the case had was that a witness recalled seeing a white Budget box truck turn the wrong way down the street just before sunrise on the day of the heist. Police decided to keep an eye on Murphy and any of his known associates, and they kept looking for clues. Eventually, they learned that Murphy had been hanging out with several younger girlfriends, many of whom only dated Murphy because he helped support their drug habits.

Four months after the heist, police were called to investigate a domestic disturbance case between Murphy and his top girlfriend, Rikkile Brown. While at the house, police discovered that one of the witnesses, another of Murphy's girlfriends named Jordayne Hartman, had a warrant out for her arrest. Hartman was arrested and brought in for questioning. She revealed that she and Murphy were on bad terms, and that she was no longer one of his favored girlfriends. She revealed that Murphy often gave his girlfriends loot from his heists, and while Brown had gotten a real Giants Super Bowl ring, Hartman had only been given one of the RadioShack rings.

THE CASE TODAY

With that information, police had enough evidence to move on Murphy. In the early morning hours of Jan 23, 2009, dozens of law enforcement officials split up to hit Murphy's home, car, and his business, North Shore Movers. At his offices, police discovered the cell phone jammer, complete with a receipt for its purchase signed by Murphy, and a list of jewelers and precious metals processing plants. E.

A. Dion was included on the list, and Murphy had written detailed notes about their phone systems in the margins next to the listing.

While police tore apart the warehouse, another team of officers searched Murphy's home. Before long, they'd found rare coins, fake IDs for Murphy, and over $10,000 in cash hidden behind radiators and inside closets. Next they found safe-deposit box keys, and when they looked inside a purse on the floor, they found a New York Giants Super Bowl ring. Murphy was in the next room over, in bed with one of his girlfriends. Police arrested him while he was still in his boxers.

With Murphy in custody, police went back to the two safe-deposit box keys and discovered that they belonged to different banks. In the first box, they discover a set of rare coins that belonged to the Dion family, and in the second, they found twenty-seven more Super Bowl rings. Next, police arrested Murphy's two accomplices, Joe Morgan, who had been the second man inside the building, and David Nassor, who served as the lookout man.

Nassor immediately made a plea deal, and Morgan agreed to plead guilty to another robbery that he and Murphy had recently pulled. In that robbery, Morgan and Murphy attempted to steal over $90 million in cash from a Brinks facility in Ohio, but accidentally set the money on fire with a tool called a thermal lance and had to settle for stealing several million dollars in coins. (See Tools of the Trade: The Thermal Lance, page 127, for more about this case gone wrong.)

Murphy stood trial first for the Ohio case and chose to defend himself in court, which went as well as you might expect. In 2011, he was found guilty and sentenced to thirteen years in federal prison. He was then sent to Boston to stand trial for the E. A. Dion case. Murphy filed a series of appeals and motions to delay the trial but eventually additional attempts to file motions to delay were rejected. Murphy again decided to represent himself in court, and in December 2019, he pleaded guilty for his part in the heist. He was sentenced to two additional years in state prison. As of this writing, Murphy is still incarcerated at the Bristol County Jail in Massachusetts.

TOOLS OF THE TRADE: THE THERMAL LANCE

Though the thermal lance might not always be practical, it is always effective.

WHAT IS IT?

A thermal lance is a cutting tool that uses extremely high temperatures to slice through anything from concrete to steel, making it a great choice when you need to get into a bank vault no matter what. Where a saw or drill may take several minutes or hours to get through tough materials, a thermal lance can accomplish the same task in seconds.

HOW DOES IT WORK?

Lances are typically made out of oxygen tanks connected to steel pipes that are packed with wires made out of aluminum, iron, or magnesium. As the oxygen flows through the pipe, it is ignited and burned up by the iron in the steel, which causes the other metals in the wires to create massive streams of sparks and hot slag, which can burn at temperatures up to 5000°F, even underwater.

THE GREAT PEARL HEIST

The world's most valuable necklace meet the world's most cunning thief.

JULY 16, 1913 ★ *EUROPE*

DESCRIPTION

Before pearls could be synthesized or farmed, their value was often equal to or greater than that of diamonds or other precious stones. In 1913, London jeweler Max Mayer purchased a strand of sixty-one flawless pink pearls whose size and color gradiented perfectly; he knew he had something truly special. Called the "Mona Lisa of pearl necklaces," this necklace was appraised to be worth twice as much as the Hope Diamond.

Mayer quickly began looking for interested buyers for the necklace, and when he was unable to find a potential buyer in London, he expanded his search to international clients. Before long, he had received word that someone in Paris was interested, and Mayer arranged to send the necklace to France so the buyer could inspect it before purchase, as was common practice at the time. Mayer received an address for the buyer and packaged

the necklace in his trademark light blue paper, which he sealed with his distinct double "M" wax seal.

With the package ready to go, Mayer sent out the world's most valuable necklace via standard post. While this might sound foolish, at the time, this was actually the safer option as private couriers were more likely to be robbed. Sending high-value items in the regular mail allowed them to hide in plain sight among potentially hundreds of identical mailbags, making it all but impossible for a thief to find specific parcels.

After the package reached the buyer in Paris, Mayer received word that the buyer was no longer interested, and that the necklace would be sent back shortly. Later that week, Mayer received his parcel. He removed the brown exterior wrapping to reveal his light blue linen paper, broke his wax seal, and gently opened the package. Instead of seeing his famed pink pearls, however, Mayer found himself looking at eleven sugar cubes wrapped in a French newspaper. His necklace was gone.

KNOWN SUSPECTS

Perhaps unsurprisingly, news of the most valuable necklace on Earth residing in London quickly reached the top of the city's criminal underground, particularly renowned thief and fence Joseph Grizzard. Grizzard was considered by many to be the most talented criminal mastermind in the world, and was a larger-than-life figure in his own time. Grizzard often threw wild parties and balls, often with police officers as invited guests, though they came to Grizzard's home in an official capacity as well.

During one of Grizzard's dinner parties, the chief of police knocked on the door and told Grizzard that he needed to search his home for a stolen diamond necklace. Grizzard obliged, and allowed the police to inspect his house while he told jokes and poured drinks for his dinner guests. When the police found nothing, they apologized for the inconvenience and left. As soon as the door shut, Grizzard went over to his seat at the dinner table, picked up his spoon, and fished the necklace out of his soup, to the delight

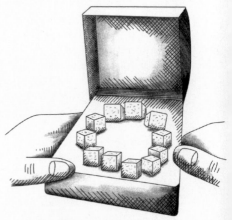

of his guests.

Naturally, when he heard about an even more expensive necklace, Grizzard quickly set a plan in motion to steal it. He enlisted the help of another notorious London thief named James Lockett. Realizing that the necklace would most likely be sent out from Mayer's office via post, they began watching the office and discovered that the same mail carrier delivered Mayer's mail each day. After following the postman for several days to determine his route, Grizzard rented an office in a building that was located toward the beginning of the carrier's route. Lockett also followed Mayer around, waiting for an indication as to when and where the necklace might be getting shipped.

Next, the thieves approached the mail carrier and offered him a bribe of £200 sterling, substantially more than his salary, in exchange for momentary access to one package in his mailbag, which the postal carrier quickly accepted. When they finally learned that the necklace was being sent out, Grizzard traveled to Paris to perform surveillance on the prospective buyer. Each time the buyer took a meeting in a café, Grizzard was nearby, drinking his coffee, reading his favorite French newspaper, and pocketing sugar cubes.

When Grizzard determined that the buyer was sending the pearls back to London, he raced back to England and notified the postman that the time was near. On the day the necklace was to be delivered back to Mayer,

the postal carrier first delivered it to the rented office at the beginning of his route, where another of Grizzard's accomplices named Simon Silverman quickly but carefully opened the package, took the pearls, and replaced them with the sugar cubes and a sheet of the French newspaper.

Once the swap was made, Silverman took out a wax seal stamp that matched Mayer's, and closed the package. When the package was ready, he gave it back to the postman right before he reached Mayer's office. Moments later, Mayer would realize he'd been robbed.

THE CASE TODAY

The investigation launched by Scotland Yard would be one of the most extensive in their history. As they sent out officers to spy on Grizzard, who was immediately a suspect, Grizzard sent out his own men to spy on those police officers. When police sent out surveillance on Grizzard's spies, the criminal mastermind responded with more spies of his own. By the time the investigation was over, the police had undercover detectives dressed in patrol officer uniforms just to throw Grizzard off.

Police set up a sting operation to buy the necklace, which was now too hot to sell, but Grizzard quickly sensed

the trap and abandoned the sale. After several months of being unable to sell the pearls, one of Grizzard's associates dumped an envelope into a drain and walked away. When police opened the envelope, they found all but three of the pearls from the necklace inside. Eventually Grizzard and his entire crew were arrested for the crime by lead detective Alfred Ward. Ward deeply respected Grizzard, and even visited him in prison and petitioned for his early release, which was eventually granted.

A NOTORIOUS NE'ER-DO-WELL

America's greatest living reformed jewel thief.

WHO: LARRY LAWTON
WHEN: 1961–PRESENT
WHERE: UNITED STATES

Lawrence "Larry" Lawton was born on October 3, 1961, in North Hempstead, New York. His father, a sheet-metal worker, sent union bribes to the New York Mafia and Larry found himself drawn to the world of organized crime. After leaving the Coast Guard, Larry started taking work as a loan shark and bookie, but within a few years, Lawton found his criminal calling: robbery.

At the age of twenty-eight, Lawton robbed his first store as part of an insurance scam, and quickly began robbing jewelry stores up and down the East Coast of the United States, using a Mafia fence on Mulberry Street in New York City's Little Italy to sell the diamonds and jewels he stole.

On December 2, 1996, Lawton was arrested by the FBI in connection with various heists. He was offered a plea deal in exchange for naming and testifying against his associates, but Lawton refused the deal and was sentenced to eleven years in prison on robbery and racketeering charges. During his time in prison, Lawton earned a paralegal degree and volunteered to become a gang mediator. He was released from prison in 2007 and began a new life as a criminal justice reform advocate and motivational speaker.

While most thieves are characterized by their crimes, Lawton has become much better known for his philanthropic work. Lawton founded the Reality Check Program and now helps deter at-risk youths from a life of crime by sharing his experiences and his regrets. He has also become a popular internet personality, creating a YouTube channel where he analyzes fictional robberies from movies and TV and answers questions about prison and the robberies he committed.

KNOWN HEISTS

Lawton is responsible for an estimated twenty to twenty-five robberies along the East Coast worth an approximate $15–$20 million in jewels, gold, and watches. Lawton's usual modus operandi was to go into a store pretending to be a customer, while scouting out the store's security and assessing where the best jewelry was located. Once he'd scouted the location and all of the details were in place, Lawton and his associates would return to the store later on to perform the robbery. Lawton and his team would tie up employees and smash display cases and grab the jewels in them before fleeing the store via a getaway driver outside.

Some of Lawton's most well-known heists include $500,000 robberies in Daytona Beach and Palm Bay, Florida.

THE HATTON GARDEN HEIST

There's no school like the Old School.

APRIL 2–5, 2015 ★ *HATTON GARDEN, LONDON, UNITED KINGDOM*

DESCRIPTION

On April 1, 2015, an enormous fire broke out beneath the streets of London's famed Hatton Garden neighborhood, causing telecom and electrical systems to short out. Hatton Garden was a quiet commercial section of London, home to several jewelers. It served as the city's diamond district, complete with a centralized vault that housed safe-deposit boxes at the Hatton Garden Safe Deposit Building for the majority of the area's jewelers. The shared mega-vault had been deemed necessary by many of the jewelers after a rash of robberies during the nineteenth century.

The building boasted several impressive security features to protect the vault, which was located in the basement. Patrons and employees entered the vault via a door that led to a staircase next to the elevator. During the day, the door was left unlocked, but after business hours, only

select security guards and building employees had access to the key. Once patrons went down the stairs, they came to a second security door that also stayed open during business hours, but at night, only the building's owner and two security guards could open it. Once that door was opened, visitors had one minute to enter a five-digit code into a keypad to prevent the vault's alarm from activating.

Beyond the keypad was a set of two sliding iron gates several feet apart that could not be opened at the same time. Opening the first gate required a four-digit security code. After the first door opened, visitors needed to walk through into the air lock, which also contained the elevator shaft behind a steel shutter, and close the first gate, at which time a security guard would open the second gate and provide access to the safe-deposit box vault, with the vault door remaining open during working hours. After hours, there was no security guard inside the air lock, and the vault was protected only by its complex series of locks and the vault's twenty-inch-thick concrete walls and steel door.

At 8:19 p.m. on April 2, the day after the fire, the Hatton Garden vault was locked ahead of the four-day banking holiday for Easter. Approximately one hour later, a man in a red wig approached the building, carrying a large duffel bag on his shoulder, which helped hide his face from the CCTV cameras. The man reached into his pocket for a set of keys and let himself into the building's front door. Once inside, he disabled all but one of the security cameras and alarms, and then headed into the basement.

Minutes later, a white van parked next to the building's fire exit. Several men dressed in gas company vests, face masks, and hard hats exited the van and unloaded several wheelie bins. Shortly after, the man in the red wig opened the fire-exit door and let them inside. Across the street, another man entered an office building to serve as a lookout, but promptly fell asleep.

Once inside, the men headed upstairs to the second floor, called the elevator, and used the hold button to keep it in place. With the elevator stuck on the second floor, they went back to the ground floor and dropped down the elevator shaft to the basement. From inside the elevator shaft, they pried open the shutters to the air lock and tried to disable that alarm as well, but accidentally triggered it instead. When building security came, they didn't see any

disturbance at the front door, assumed it was a false alarm, and left. Inside, the thieves began working to open the second air lock door, which led to the vault door.

They set up an enormous drill, a Hilti DD350, anchored it to the vault wall, and connected a hose to reduce dust and prevent overheating. Over the next two hours, the thieves drilled three ten-inch-wide holes into the vault wall, slightly overlapping them to create one hole wide enough to crawl through. Before they could get in, though, they needed to clear a final obstacle; the safe-deposit boxes themselves. The steel cabinets were bolted into the concrete they'd just drilled through, so the thieves set up a hydraulic ram to push the boxes far enough away from the hole to let them get inside.

Once the ram was set up, the thieves turned it on and after a few minutes of pushing, it stopped working. With progress halted, the thieves packed up for the night and left just after 8:00 a.m. on April 3. One of the gang's ringleaders took this as a bad sign and quit, but the rest of the gang rested and the next day, two of the thieves went to a hardware store to buy a new hydraulic ram. At approximately 10:00 p.m. on the night of April 4, the crew, minus their leader, headed back to the Hatton Garden Safe Deposit Building with the new ram. After discovering that the fire exit

door had been locked again, another one of the thieves quit the heist.

After contacting the man in the red wig, known only as "Basil," to reopen the door, the thieves got back downstairs to the vault and quickly set up the new ram. Less than an hour later, it had pushed the safe-deposit boxes off the wall, toppling them to the floor. Basil and another of the thieves slid into the vault through the hole, but the rest of the thieves were too large to fit through the narrow opening. The two men inside the vault began smashing open safe-deposit boxes using sledgehammers and angle grinders to work as quickly as they could. Once the boxes were opened, the contents were sent back through the hole to the other thieves, who loaded up their wheelie bins with the haul, as well as their tools and any evidence.

At approximately 5:45 a.m. on April 5, the thieves left the crime scene. They'd managed to break into a total of seventy-three of the vault's 999 boxes, and now had a haul of gold, diamonds, gems, and cash worth approximately $200 million. The thieves cleaned up the site, ensured they hadn't left any DNA evidence behind, and then loaded the bins back into their van before getting into a white Mercedes, which dropped each of them off at their homes.

KNOWN SUSPECTS

The theft was discovered two days later, when the Hatton Garden Safe Deposit Building reopened for business. By this time, the bandits had already met and divided their ill-gotten gains amongst themselves, a process called "The Slaughter" by many thieves. Scotland Yard's specialized robbery division, The Flying Squadron, immediately assigned fifty officers to the case. Convinced that this was an inside job, the Flying Squadron conducted extensive interviews of the building's employees, but soon realized they were no closer to catching the thieves.

Next, they reviewed security camera footage and spotted the thieves entering the white Mercedes. Investigators found the car's license plate on other security cameras around London. Before long, they had traced the car's movement to the hardware store where the thieves purchased the second hydraulic ram, and to the home of the car's owner, Kenny Collins. Collins, aged seventy-four, was the gang's sleepy lookout and driver.

The Flying Squadron went to the hardware store and found a purchase order for the ram signed by a "Vinnie" Jones. The name was a joking nod to the famous British actor by the same name, but the purchaser, Doug Jones, had listed his real home address on the form. With Collins and Jones identified, detectives began comparing their phone records and identified several numbers that had been in contact with each other immediately before and after the heist.

With the owners of the phone numbers identified, police installed trackers on the suspects' cars, photographed them at their homes, and began following them to local pubs where they often talked openly about performing the heist with each other. While police had originally suspected middle-aged men, all of the thieves were elderly criminals, the youngest of whom was fifty-seven. Detectives continued to gather evidence, but waited to arrest the thieves until they had the loot in hand. Finally, police got their break when they heard the men talk about their plans to melt down gold the following day.

On May 19, the Flying Squad detectives stormed twelve locations simultaneously and arrested the entire band of geriatric thieves. Collins and Jones were arrested with another man named Terry Perkins, as they were setting up a smelter to melt down gold worth $5 million. The gang's ringleader, Brian Reader, then seventy-six years old, was arrested, despite having quit in the middle of the heist. Reader, a career criminal, had previously been arrested for his involvement in the $145 million Brinks-mat heist in 1983.

A few weeks later, detectives arrested a man named Carl Wood. Wood was one of the men that had climbed through the hole into the vault and had evaded police for his part in the heist; instead, he was arrested for torturing a money launderer. The police also arrested the gang's fence, a criminal known as Billy the Fish. Despite the rest of the gang being in custody, police could not find the man in the red wig, Basil.

THE CASE TODAY

For his limited role during the heist, Reader was sentenced to just over six years in prison for moving stolen goods. He died in prison in 2018. The rest of the bandits received seven-year sentences.

Three years after the heist, Basil's identity was revealed to be Michael Seed, a known figure in the British underworld. On March 28, 2018, Seed was arrested and charged with burglary and conspiracy to commit burglary. He was found guilty of both and sentenced to concurrent sentences of ten and eight years.

Due to the secretive nature of safe-deposit boxes, the true value of the heist will likely never be known. Police have provided ranges of $14 million to $200 million for the gold, diamonds, cash, and bonds, though it is likely that the total value of the robbery was significantly higher. As of 2021, only $4 million has been recovered.

LAW ENFORCEMENT LEGENDS

Scotland Yard's most tenacious thief takers.

WHO: THE FLYING SQUAD
WHEN: 1919–PRESENT
WHERE: UNITED KINGDOM

In the early twentieth century, as robberies became more popular and more sophisticated, law enforcement was forced to evolve as well, to maintain order. While beat cops could certainly help with purse snatchers, there was a growing need for a dedicated force that specialized in catching thieves, and with that goal in mind, London's Scotland Yard formed an experimental team known as the Flying Squadron.

Originally the task force was called the Mobile Patrol Experiment and consisted of a dozen officers who used a specialized carriage with hidden observation holes to observe pickpockets in the act or to perform surveillance on known and suspected thieves. After the program proved to be a success, the team was upgraded to permanent status and recruited some people that had spent World War I tracking down German spies and building dossiers on them. These specialists compiled similar files on

some of London's most cunning thieves. The team was allowed to operate throughout all of the London metropolitan area without regard to jurisdiction, so the task force became known as "The Flying Squad" due to their ability to seemingly "fly" over jurisdiction boundaries.

Over the next several decades, the Flying Squad continued to grow in both size and scope. Squad members employed a vast network of criminal informants, usually consisting of thieves that the squad had arrested and offered reduced sentences to in exchange for cooperation. This would later lead to corruption and bribery controversies, but did let the Flying Squad quickly solve some of England's biggest robberies. Arguably even more importantly, it allowed Scotland Yard to stay a step ahead of some of the biggest attempted heists in London and catch the thieves in the act in remarkably brazen operations.

KNOWN HEIST ARRESTS

In one such operation, in 1948, the Flying Squad received a tip that thieves planned to steal nearly $1 million in gold and jewels from a secure warehouse at Heathrow International Airport. After learning that the thieves planned to drug the guards, Flying Squad members replaced the guards for their shift on the night of the heist and pretended to be drugged. After the thieves went to grab the safe keys off one of the "unconscious" officers, police sprang into action and a violent battle broke out, severely wounding several officers and thieves, before all nine thieves were arrested.

The Flying Squad has investigated many of England's most notorious heists, including the Great Train Robbery of 1963, the 1993 Barclays Bank Robbery (which was the first time that police were fired on by robbers with automatic weapons), and the Hatton Garden Heist. They also took down the infamous London gangsters the Kray Twins.

Perhaps the Flying Squad's most well-known bust was during 2000's daring Millennium Dome Heist. Famed diamond company De Beers had organized a massive exhibition with thousands of diamonds and jewels on display, the most notable of which was the Millennium Star. The Millennium Star was a flawless 203-carat diamond worth approximately $200 million, and is widely considered to be one of the most beautiful and perfect gems on earth. The Flying Squad received a tip that the expo was being targeted for a heist.

On the morning of November 7, 2000, a team of thieves armed with smoke grenades, nail guns, and sledgehammers drove an excavator through the security fence and the external wall of the Millennium Dome, just outside of what was called "the money zone," where the diamonds were being held. Once inside, the thieves started throwing the smoke bombs and using the nail guns to weaken the bulletproof glass display cases. Once the glass looked sufficiently weak, they used the sledgehammers to break through the cases and steal the diamonds.

Before the thieves could get to the stones though, the Flying Squad jumped into action. Several officers had been hiding behind false walls in anticipation for the heist, and others had pretended to be custodial staff, with their weapons hidden in garbage cans or under their jumpsuits. While the four would-be thieves were arrested in the dome, police also apprehended a speedboat driver on the Thames who was preparing to act as the getaway driver, as well as another man across the river who had precisely been monitoring police frequencies and serving as a lookout.

Ultimately, ten people were arrested for their connection to the attempted heist. The Flying Squad's efficiency is one of the reasons the group is known in the underworld as "The Thief Takers."

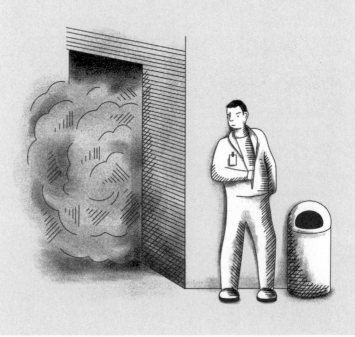

* * *

TOOLS OF THE TRADE: THE DRILL PRESS

WHAT IS IT?

AS SAFES AND VAULTS HAVE GOTTEN MORE ADVANCED, ONE TOOL HAS BECOME INCREASINGLY MORE IMPORTANT FOR THIEVES SINCE THE 1900S: THE DRILL PRESS. DRILLING INTO SAFES TENDS TO SERVE ONE OF A FEW PURPOSES: GETTING A GLIMPSE INSIDE AT THE SAFE'S CONTENTS, REVEALING THE INTERNAL MECHANISMS OF THE SAFE DIAL, OR DRILLING DIRECTLY INTO THE FACE OF A LOCK TO MOVE INTERNAL LEVERS OR DRIVE CAMS OUT OF THE LOCKING POSITION VIA A PUNCH ROD. WHICHEVER METHOD THIEVES EMPLOY, THE DRILL MUST BE PRECISELY PLACED, WHICH IS WHERE THE DRILL PRESSES COME IN.

HOW DOES IT WORK?

DRILL PRESSES CAN BE ATTACHED DIRECTLY TO SAFES OR VAULT DOORS VIA STRONG MAGNETS. OR, FOR LARGER JOBS LIKE THE HATTON GARDEN HEIST, INDUSTRIAL-SIZED DRILL PRESSES CAN BE PUT IN PLACE VIA JACK STANDS. DRILL PRESSES OPERATE LIKE TRADITIONAL DRILLS, BUT WITH AN ADDITIONAL SET OF GUIDE RAILS THAT ALLOW FOR EXTREMELY ACCURATE DRILLING BOTH IN TERMS OF THE PATH THE DRILL BIT WILL TAKE AND THE DEPTH. THIS IS CRUCIAL WHEN TRYING TO CRACK SAFES WITH ANTI-THEFT FEATURES LIKE GLASS PLATES AND RE-LOCKERS, WHICH SNAP THE LOCKING MECHANISMS INTO PLACE IF TAMPERING IS DETECTED.

THE CARLTON CANNES HEIST

The biggest heist in France's history.

DESCRIPTION

Just before 11:30 a.m. on July 28, 2013, at the Carlton hotel in Cannes, France, preparations were underway for the "Extraordinary Diamonds" showcase for famed Israeli jeweler Leviev. The Carlton seemed to be the ideal location for a show like this: posh, beautiful, and historic. The hotel had served as the setting for the classic Hitchcock film *To Catch a Thief*, wherein Cary Grant plays a diamond thief who steals from the hotel's wealthy guests.

Several bags full of diamonds, necklaces, watches, and other jewels were taken from the hotel's vault into the main salon, where they were put into secure display cases for the duration of the show. As the jewels made their way to the salon, a man entered the area through an open French window.

Wearing gloves and using a bandanna and motorcycle helmet to cover his face, he pulled out an automatic pistol from his jacket and waved it in the air at the show's vendors and the three security guards, all of whom were unarmed. Without firing a shot, the thief grabbed a bag containing a briefcase and a small box and ran out the other side of the show room, jumping out of another large window onto the street a few feet below. Once he hit the road, he ran from the hotel and made his escape on foot. He was not followed.

In just under a minute, he had pulled off the most valuable heist in French history. Inside the bag he'd stolen were seventy-two pieces of jewelry and loose stones, thirty-four of which had been graded as "Exceptional," due to their incredible clarity and total lack of color. In total, the heist took nearly $136 million.

KNOWN SUSPECTS

Due to the thief's face being hidden by a motorcycle helmet and the speed of the heist itself, police have never been able to conclusively identify the culprit. Because he entered through the only window where the jewels were vulnerable, after they'd been moved from the hotel's vault to the exhibition room, but before they'd been locked inside secure display cases, investigators do not believe that he acted alone. The timing suggests that the thief had an inside source that tipped him off to when the jewels were being moved and when they would be relatively unprotected by unarmed guards and jewelers.

Police suspect that the heist could have been pulled off by the legendary international jewel thieves known as

The Pink Panthers. Two days before the heist, Milan Poparic, a known Pink Panther, had escaped from a Swiss prison during a coordinated attack on the jail, and two other Panthers had broken free in the prior month.

Another popular theory was that the crime was orchestrated by the jeweler hosting the exhibition, Lev Leviev. He controled all aspects of the diamond life cycle from mining to final sale. Leviev would be able to recut and resell the diamonds, while still collecting insurance money for the theft. He was one of the few people who knew exactly what time the diamonds would be out of the vault and easier to steal.

THE CASE TODAY

Currently, no arrests have been made in connection to the heist. Tragically, shortly after one of Lev Leviev's accountants was questioned by police regarding the crime, she fell ten stories to her death in Moscow.

There is a reward of $1.3 million for the return of the stones.

ONE OF THE WORST HEISTS OF ALL TIME

This heist went up in smoke.

WHAT: THE BURNING BRINKS DEPOT
WHEN: JANUARY 2009
WHERE: COLUMBUS, OHIO, UNITED STATES

In January 2009, a team of professional thieves cut through the fence of a Brinks cash warehouse and climbed to the building's roof. One of them set up a cell phone jammer and cut the building's telephone lines, while another disabled security cameras on the roof. The men cut holes into the roof and used ropes to rappel down to the floor two stories below. Once inside the building, the thieves grabbed a forklift to move a Brinks armored truck away from the loading bay door and backed their box truck into the warehouse.

They unloaded their supplies from the truck and headed for the vault door. The vault door was too complex for traditional safecracking techniques to work fast enough, but the thieves had another plan to get through the door. Literally. They grabbed the oxygen tanks they'd stored in the truck and assembled a series of magnesium rods, creating a burglar tool known as a thermal lance, which superheated the rods hot enough to cut through the vault door or anything else they might encounter. While two of the thieves assembled the lance, a third man destroyed the surveillance camera system.

WHAT WENT WRONG

Before long, the thermal lance cut a hole in the vault door nearly large enough for one of the men to crawl through. On the other side of the vault door, over $90 million in cash began to smoke and smolder due to the extreme heat. When the thieves could no longer see inside the vault due to the smoke, they moved a box fan to the hole and started it up in an attempt to clear out the smoke. Instead, the increased air flow caused the money to burn even faster, acting like a billow.

The thieves panicked and hurriedly sprayed a fire extinguisher into the vault, and then ran a hose through the hole to fight the flames. The combination of acrid smoke and panic caused one of the thieves to vomit into a bucket. The most experienced of the thieves forced his body through the hole in the vault door and tried to grab whatever cash he could, but the fire, water, and extinguishers had ruined almost everything inside. Determined not to leave empty-handed, the thieves used forklifts to move several pallets full of coins into the back of their box truck. When they had taken everything they could, they collected their equipment, loaded everything into the truck, and drove off just before 8:00 a.m. with nearly $3 million in coins and salvageable cash. Right before leaving, they used epoxy to glue all of the building's exterior doors closed.

KNOWN SUSPECTS

When police arrived at the scene, they realized that the heist must have been the work of professionals. Jamming cell phones, cutting phone lines, and rappelling in from the roof sounded all too familiar to another high-profile heist that had been in the news recently: the theft of the New York Giants' Super Bowl rings. Police reached out to authorities working on that case and spoke to a recently arrested informant, who told police that he'd been told to perform recon on the Brinks warehouse earlier by the mastermind of both heists, Sean Murphy.

Murphy led a team of Boston-area thieves known as the "Lynn Breakers" because they were mostly from Lynn, Masachusetts. He was notorious for his use of cell phone jammers and was arrested less than a week after the Brinks heist for his role in both robberies. The other two thieves, Joseph Morgan and Robert Doucette, were also arrested and pleaded guilty to conspiracy and transportation of stolen goods across state lines. Morgan received four-and-a-half years in prison for his role in the heist. Doucette received two years in prison in exchange for testifying against Murphy. Murphy received thirteen years for his role in both heists.

THE BRITISH CROWN JEWELS HEIST

The world's most famous jewels are no match for one man's spite.

MAY 1671 ★ *LONDON, ENGLAND*

DESCRIPTION

In April 1671, a man wearing a parson's robes entered the Tower of London with a female companion to view the newly crafted crown jewels. The couple paid the elderly master of the Jewel House, Talbot Edwards, their admission fees. Moments later, the woman began complaining of a stomach pain and asked the seventy-seven year old Edwards if she could have something to drink. The elderly man's wife invited the couple into their chambers to rest until comfortable, and before long, both couples formed a fast friendship.

The parson and his wife visited the custodians of the Jewel House frequently and eventually began arranging a marriage between the Parson's nephew and the Edward's daughter. On May 9, 1671, the parson brought his nephew to the Tower of London to meet the Edwards family

for dinner. While the food was being prepared, the Parson asked if Edwards could arrange a private viewing of the crown jewels for himself, his nephew, and two friends they'd brought along. Edwards agreed and led them down into the Jewel House.

Once the men entered the Jewel House, the door was closed and one of the men threw a cloak over Edwards and hit him with a hammer. Edwards was knocked to the ground, tied up, and gagged before being stabbed by one of the men. The other men removed the metal grill protecting the jewels and then took the treasure from the display case. Upon realizing that St. Edward's Crown was too bulky to hide, the parson used the hammer to smash and flatten it until it could be stored discreet beneath his robes. Another man tried to hide the scepter and cross in his trousers but couldn't

make it fit until he filed the scepter in half. Another thief grabbed the Sovereign's Orb and also stashed it in his trousers.

The thieves then ran for their horses, dropping the scepter in the process. Edwards managed to remove his gag and began yelling "Treason! Murder! The Crown is stolen!" Tower guards sprang into action while the thieves attempted to ride their horses out of the Tower before the iron gate could be closed, but they were unsuccessful and quickly captured.

KNOWN SUSPECTS

Unsurprisingly, the parson had not been a member of the clergy as he claimed but was instead revealed to be Colonel Thomas Blood. Blood had been born to a respectable family in County Clare, Ireland, in 1618 and had been educated in England before returning home to Ireland. When the English Civil War began in 1642, Blood enlisted to fight for King Charles I, but later switched sides and fought as a lieutenant in Oliver Cromwell's ranks. Cromwell rewarded Blood's service by providing him with land grants and a title, but when King Charles II assumed power, Blood was forced to return to Ireland with his family.

Blood was driven to bankruptcy by King Charles II's Settlement Act of 1652 and vowed to become an insurrectionist against the crown. After a pair of failed kidnapping attempts against the Duke of Ormonde, Blood instead decided to steal the crown jewels, which had been crafted for Charles II after the previous crown jewels had been stolen and destroyed.

THE CASE TODAY

While in jail, Blood refused to speak to anybody but King Charles II himself. Eventually, the king agreed, and Blood was taken to the royal palace in chains. King Charles questioned Blood about the theft, telling him that the usual penalty for the theft of something so valuable was death. When the king claimed that the Crown Jewels had cost over £100,000 to re-create, Blood reportedly laughed and said that they were barely worth £6,000.

When the king asked what Blood would do with his life if he should be allowed to live, Blood told the king that he "would endeavor to deserve it, Sire!" King Charles II decided not only to allow Blood to live but also set him free and granted him a pardon and land in Ireland. Edwards survived his attack and was promised a sum of £300 for his service protecting the Jewel House, though the payment was never made.

THE ANTWERP DIAMOND HEIST

The world's largest and most impressive diamond heist ever.

FEBRUARY 15–16, 2003 ★ *ANTWERP, BELGIUM*

DESCRIPTION

Antwerp is one of the largest cities in Belgium and has a population of a little over half a million people. It's also home to the Antwerp Diamond Center, one of the largest hubs for diamond merchants in the world. The Diamond Center is a series of buildings that cover approximately one square mile and handle over $50 billion in transactions each year. Approximately 80 percent of the world's rough diamonds pass through the Antwerp Diamond Center, though it's important to note that this is just what's documented.

The diamond district also boasts an impenetrable vault with ten layers of security that houses approximately 160 safe-deposit boxes that are rented out by various diamond merchants.

One of these safe-deposit boxes was rented by Leonardo Notarbartolo, an Italian man who also rented an office in the district. Notarbartolo was a career thief, and Antwerp was an ideal location for him to be able to

have access to his various black-market contacts when he needed to fence stolen goods. Leonardo committed his first theft at the age of six when his mother sent him to a market for milk. When he arrived, the shopkeeper was asleep, and so Leonardo decided to just help himself to the cash in the register. From that point on, he was hooked. He learned how to steal cars, pick locks, and establish contacts for all aspects of criminal activity. He had a tunnel guy, a guy that could climb buildings, and an electronics guy. He had a specialist for everything, and he called his band of thieves the School of Turin.

Twice a month or so, Notarbartolo would leave his family in Turin, Italy, and head to Antwerp to make his sales with a few trusted merchants. On one of his trips, one of his dealers approached him, and said that he wanted to hire Notarbartolo for a big job: he wanted to rob the Diamond Center, and he needed to know if it was possible.

Notarbartolo told him that it was almost certainly not possible, but the dealer offered him $100,000 to think about it and give him a definitive answer. Notarbartolo was pretty familiar with the vault because he'd rented a safe-deposit box there for years, and he was well aware of the incredibly complex security measures that the vault employed. It utilized a security principle called Defense in Depth, which consists of multiple layers of security working together. The Antwerp vault's security included:

A one-foot-thick vault door that weighed three tons and had a combination wheel with 100,000,000 possible combinations.

Thermal sensors.

Seismic sensors inside the vault door; drilling wasn't an option.

Motion detectors.

Light sensors inside the vault.

Over sixty cameras pointed at the vault door that linked directly to the guard station and were saved on tape.

Magnetic sensors on the vault door and frame that would activate an alarm if they were separated (which happened if the vault door opened).

A foot-long key that was almost impossible to duplicate.

Guards that inspected the badges of each person coming in and out during business hours.

A second steel grate that needed to be opened to finally provide access to the vault.

Once inside the vault, a thief still needed to get into the deposit boxes, and each box had a lock with over 17,000 possible combinations. During the day, the vault door was left open so that clients could access their deposit boxes at will. Notarbartolo did a recon run to his box, wearing a pen camera in his shirt pocket, and entered the vault. He had to give his access card to the guards, and when he got to the metal grate at the vault door, he had to be buzzed in electronically by the guards who watched him enter the vault on their cameras. His pen camera snapped hundreds of photos of the entire process. At night, there were no guards because the diamond center trusted the other nine layers of security to keep thieves out.

Notarbartolo also trusted the security of the vault and told the dealer that the job couldn't be done. Five months later, the dealer reached out to him again and asked him to come to a warehouse. When Notarbartolo arrived, the dealer took him inside and Notarbartolo found himself in an exact replica of the bank vault. The photos from his pen camera had proven to be good enough to build an uncanny duplicate, and inside the vault were three men.

The men, known only by their nicknames, introduced themselves. First was The Monster, an enormous Italian man who was both tall and muscular. He was a getaway driver, lock picker, and electronics expert. Next was The Genius. He specialized in alarm systems. Next, a quiet old man introduced himself as The King of Keys. Like his name implied, he was an expert locksmith and key forger. He told Notarbartolo to obtain a clear video of the foot-long vault key, and he'd handle the rest. Finally, there was Speedy, who had no skills.

The men talked and started walking through the job, practicing everything they could in the replica vault. Notarbartolo took tiny cameras with him as he went into the real vault to access his safe-deposit boxes, placing the cameras in strategic locations so they could perform reconnaissance.

After months of preparation and practice, they were ready. On Friday, February 14, Notarbartolo entered the vault one last time before the heist, doing one final walk-through. Before he left this time, he took a travel-size bottle of hairspray and sprayed a light coat on the thermal and motion sensors, creating a film that made them unable to detect body heat or motion.

He chose February 14 because it was a Jewish holy day, which would ensure that the Jewish diamond merchants wouldn't go to the Diamond Center. He parked across the street and the Monster, the King of Keys, Speedy, and the Genius exited the car carrying large duffel bags.

They approached a small office building adjacent to the Diamond Center, and the King of Keys picked the lock. Once inside, they exited through the rear of the building and found themselves in a courtyard that was shared by the back of the Diamond Center. The Genius grabbed a ladder that he'd stored previously and made his way up to a balcony on the second floor. There was a camera/heat sensor around the corner, but the Genius used a polyester shield to slowly approach the sensor, disabling it with a bag.

The rest of the crew, save for Notarbartolo (who was still in the car), made their way up the ladder and through a window that the Genius had opened after disabling the window alarms. Once inside, they headed downstairs until they were two stories underground at the vault.

Next, it was time to break into the "impossible vault" with its nine layers of security. The Genius pulled out two aluminum plates, affixed them with double-sided tape, and then stuck them to the magnetic sensors. Next, he removed the screws holding the sensors in place and stuck the magnetic sensors to the side of the vault wall, still touching because of the aluminum plates. They entered the four-digit vault combination, which they discovered thanks to the security cameras that Notorbartolo had set up.

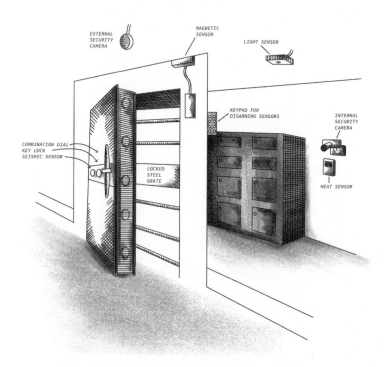

EXTERNAL SECURITY CAMERA

MAGNETIC SENSOR

LIGHT SENSOR

KEYPAD FOR DISARMING SENSORS

INTERNAL SECURITY CAMERA

COMBINATION DIAL

KEY LOCK

SEISMIC SENSOR

LOCKED STEEL GRATE

HEAT SENSOR

The King of Keys had created a duplicate of the foot-long key, but never needed to use it, because the real one was just hanging in a closet next to the vault! Using the real key, they opened up the vault door, and the King of Keys picked the lock to the final metal gate.

They were in.

The Monster slowly approached the motion and heat sensors and covered them with a Styrofoam shield, because he didn't want to risk the hairspray wearing off. He put a piece of black tape over the light sensor, and

then slipped a bag over the cameras. Finally, he found the security system wires in the ceiling, and installed a bypass, rendering the alarms useless while still making them appear to be active. The thieves were now free to rob the vault and they went to work breaking open safe-deposit boxes.

They used a small, hand-operated drill made by the King of Keys. He inserted a small strip of metal into the drill, then put it in a lock, and started spinning the drill until the lock snapped open. As he worked on the locks, the rest of the men would empty the boxes. Speedy was acting as an inside lookout man, but his phone didn't work in the vault, so he went back to the ground level and stayed in phone contact with Notarbartolo.

By 5:30 a.m., they'd opened over one hundred boxes, all in complete darkness, and had filled their duffel bags with gold and silver bars, tons of international currencies, and leather satchels filled with rough and finished diamonds. Most importantly, they took the paperwork to go with the diamonds so they could be sold legitimately.

The thieves had so much loot that it took them almost an hour to get it all out of the vault and into the car. Once the car was loaded, Notarbartolo drove off and the other four men made their way on foot to Notarbartolo's apartment. Within a half hour, all five men were in his living room, and they began checking out their loot like kids dumping their Halloween haul out on the table. But as the thieves opened up the leather satchels, they were disappointed to discover that most of them were actually empty. Instead of a $100 million payday, the haul in front of them looked to be worth closer to $20 million.

They divided up what loot there was and ate some salami sandwiches. A few hours later, Notarbartolo and Speedy drove back to Turin together with a garbage bag full of evidence in the back seat. Before long, Speedy panicked, demanding that they pull over to get rid of the evidence immediately. Eventually, Speedy convinced Notarbartolo to pull off the road along a remote farm path bordering a forest. It was dark now.

Notarbartolo prepared to burn the evidence, but before he could get the garbage into the fire, Speedy emptied the bag into the wind, scattering trash all around. Before long, there was paper everywhere: security tape hanging off of branches, loose money on the ground, even half a sandwich. The men drove off, confident that the area was too remote for the trash to ever be found.

The area was remote, but unfortunately for Notarbartolo, it was a popular spot to dump trash. The property owner had been dealing with trash dumpers for quite a while, so when he saw more garbage on his land, he called the police and they immediately knew where to look. Typically, they took their time responding to these calls, but when the property owner mentioned seeing envelopes that said "Antwerp Diamond Center," the police responded quickly.

KNOWN SUSPECTS

Before long, the police had gathered large amounts of evidence, and even some gems that had been strewn about. But they couldn't find any trace of who committed the crime until they were able to piece together a receipt for a low light security camera, purchased by one Leonardo Notarbartolo and a business card for a man named Elio D'Onorio, who was most likely The Genius.

Police bagged up the evidence, including the half-eaten sandwich and a package of Antipasto Italiano Salami, and passed it on to forensics. A few days later, they raided Notarbartolo's apartment in Antwerp. They found a receipt for the salami with a time stamp that shows it was purchased right before the heist. After reviewing security footage from a store near the Diamond Center, they saw a very tall man purchase the salami: the Monster.

Meanwhile, the gang had regrouped at a bar outside of Milan, waiting for the Dealer to arrive. They had some questions for him, like why were so many diamonds missing? Was this a scam? They'd been promised eight figures each, but now were looking at closer to $3 million payouts.

Perhaps not surprisingly, the dealer never showed up.

Notarbartolo made his way back to Antwerp, with his wife, to return the rental car. He planned on showing his face at the Diamond Center the next day to remove suspicion. As they drove north, police raided his home in Turin. Notarbartolo's son Marco tried calling his parents to tip them off, but the phone was on silent mode in his father's pocket. They continued on to Antwerp and the next morning, Notarbartolo went into the Diamond Center. The security guard there knew that police were looking for him, so as soon as he saw Notarbartolo, he dialed the cops.

Before long, Notarbartolo was face-to-face with a few detectives, who kept asking him questions. Every time they spoke to him, he'd stall as long as possible to answer. He pretended to have a problem with French, and claimed he couldn't remember his address number, just how to walk there. Eventually, he led the police to his apartment. As the police car carrying Notarbartolo and the detectives pulled in front of the apartment, Notarbartolo's wife and some friends were stepping out of the building. One had a rolled-up carpet under his arm, and several had multiple bags. If Notarbartolo had stalled for even five more minutes, they probably could have been gone. Instead, the bags were found to have critical evidence, like SIM cards that were only used to call three Italian numbers: Elio D'onorio (the Genius), Ferdinando Finotto (the Monster), and Speedy (a man by the name of Pietro Tavano).

On the same day as the arrest, police found a safe in Notarbartolo's home in Turin. It contained seventeen finished diamonds, complete with paperwork linking them to Antwerp. The rolled-up carpet was vacuumed, and several more gems were found in the dustbin.

THE CASE TODAY

Notarbartolo went to trial and was found guilty. He was sentenced to ten years in prison to make an example of him. He never provided the names of his accomplices, but Donorio, Finotto, and Speedy were each sentenced to five years for their alleged roles. The King of Keys was never found or identified, but police do have some traces of DNA and cell phone records proving he did in fact exist.

LOCKED IN THE VAULT

Bank vaults are like prison cells, and if you're not careful you can get stuck in both.

WHO: FATIMA MILANOVIC
WHEN: MARCH 18, 2017
WHERE: BOCA RATON, FLORIDA

When Bobby Yampolsky, the owner of ECJ Luxe Collection in Boca Raton, received a call from a woman claiming to represent an anonymous buyer, the jeweler saw the potential for a big deal. The buyer was apparently interested in acquiring several high-quality diamonds to be used for future pieces, and over the next several weeks, the woman and Yampolsky worked out a deal for eleven diamonds to be purchased for $6.7 million. The only step left was for the buyer's representative to inspect the diamonds and complete the purchase.

On March 18, 2017, the buyer's representative entered the store. The woman was smartly dressed and confident, and was quickly greeted by Yampolsky and taken to a vault room where high-value purchases were handled. Once Yampolsky and the buyer were seated at a table in the vault, he asked if she would like to inspect the stones. She agreed, and Yampolsky pulled out an envelope and placed the diamonds onto a velvet viewing pad. After several attempted distractions, the woman looked at each stone in her hand, smiled, and agreed to the deal.

She pulled packing material from her bag and insisted the stones be wrapped up in the packaging that she provided. Yampolsky told her that wouldn't be an issue and that he would go wrap the diamonds for her. He got up, walked out of the vault, and immediately closed it, locking the woman inside, and called police.

KNOWN SUSPECTS

When police arrived, the woman, identified as Fatima Milanovic, was still inside the vault. Yampolsky explained to police that she'd attempted to distract him several times while the diamonds were out, which made him suspicious. When she insisted on having the stones wrapped in her own packing materials, Yampolsky realized that she was planning on swapping the parcel with an identically packaged one in her bag. His suspicions were confirmed when he locked her in the vault and saw her try to make a phone call before pulling out a parcel from her bag and tearing it to shreds.

When police opened the vault, they found the torn scraps of paper and a set of fake diamonds in her bag that perfectly matched the stones Yampolsky planned to sell. Milanovic was arrested for grand theft and organized fraud, and booked into Palm Beach County Jail.

WHAT WENT WRONG

While Milanovic did many things to raise suspicion, like constantly attempting to distract Yampolsky, it was ultimately something Milanovic didn't do that prompted the call to the police. Milanovic inspected the stones with only her naked eye and didn't even bring basic tools, such as a diamond tester or jeweler's loupe, to examine the diamonds. No real buyer would agree to pay millions of dollars for diamonds without subjecting them to intense examination. When Milanovic agreed to the purchase without so much as making sure the stones were real, Yampolsky knew something was wrong and locked the would-be thief in the vault.

THE HARRY WINSTON PARIS HEISTS

Two heists are twice as nice.

OCTOBER 6, 2007, AND DECEMBER 4, 2008 ★ *PARIS, FRANCE*

DESCRIPTION

On the morning of October 6, 2007, four thieves huddled in the stairwell of Harry Winston Paris, where they'd spent the night. Just before 10:00 a.m., the store's import-export director, Anne-Marie Capdeville, arrived at the store and met with the security guard to unlock the store's side door and deactivate the main alarm for the day. Capdeville went upstairs to her third-floor office, and the thieves crouched silently behind a door, waiting for her to enter. The thieves rushed her and grabbed her throat. They pinned her head to her desk and pulled out guns and batons, demanding to know how many other staff members were in the building.

Capdeville told them that only the security guard had come in with her, and two of the thieves went to find him. The guard was caught unaware in the restroom and knocked over the head with one of the batons.

As the two thieves moved the guard to his desk, the other two thieves carried Capdeville to the bathroom and bound her hands and feet before leaving her on the floor. They rejoined the other thieves at the security guard's post, where they watched the cameras and waited for more employees to arrive. Minutes later, the store's manager and two hostesses entered the store. The hostesses were immediately grabbed, searched for phones, and taken to the bathroom and tied up with Capdeville.

The manager was taken to the store's safe and ordered to open it. When the manager couldn't remember the safe combination, the thieves grabbed another employee and made her enter the safe's code into the keypad. The safe clicked open, and the thieves began emptying the jewels into bags. The hostess was then taken to another safe and ordered to open it. When this one was opened, the thieves loaded watches and other jewelry into the bags. One of the thieves yelled "Farid, there's no more time!" to a thief whose large nose protruded from his ski mask. The employees were rounded up and taken to the bathroom. As one thief grabbed the store's security camera tapes, the others sprayed the hostages with mace and ran out the store's back exit, where their getaway car was waiting. In total, they'd made off with nearly five hundred pieces of jewelry.

Investigators scoured the store looking for clues, but quickly discovered that the thieves had been incredibly careful not to leave any usable evidence. Even the stairwell where the thieves spent the night had been sprayed by a fire extinguisher, destroying any possible DNA or finger-prints. The only clues the police had were that one of the thieves had been called Farid, and another thief was referred to as "Voldemort." Police continued to follow leads, but the case quickly grew cold.

Just over a year later, on December 4, 2008, Harry's was robbed again. Just after 5:00 p.m., four men—three of them dressed as women, complete with high heels and stockings—approached the front door of the jewelry store. Once they were at the front door, the security guard glanced over and buzzed them inside, where one of the store's hostesses took them up the stairs to a private showroom. As the men entered the staircase, they pulled out guns and a hand grenade and burst into the manager's office, threat-

ening to shoot anyone who didn't cooperate.

Employees were wrangled to a central location, and then the thieves began taking them individually around the store to open display cases and deactivate alarms. The thieves continued to threaten the employees, shouting the home addresses and names of the shop workers, to instill enough fear to dissuade them from cooperating with authorities after the heist. The thieves moved from display case to display case, dumping watches and gems into a rolling suitcase before moving to the store's main safe. Once the safe was opened, the thieves removed a false bottom and grabbed a thirty-one-carat diamond ring worth over $8 million. Once the safe was emptied, the thieves fled from the store with a haul that contained nearly three hundred gems and over one hundred watches. The heist took less than twenty minutes to complete and was one of the most expensive in French history.

KNOWN SUSPECTS

Police immediately assumed that both heists were connected and suspected them to be the work of an international gang of thieves known as the Pink Panthers, who specialized in high-value heists. Fortunately, the second heist left them significantly more evidence to work with, including fingerprints left on one of the purses carried by the thieves. Because of the speed of this heist, the thieves hadn't been able to remove the security camera tapes, so when police reviewed footage from them, they noticed that the thieves did not attack one security guard, Mouloud Djennad. He was allowed to move around the store at his leisure, and he made no attempt to stop the heist or alert police.

Investigators looked into Djennad's schedule and discovered that he had also been the security guard that locked the store the night before the first heist. With Djennad pinned as the heists' inside man, police noticed his strange spending habits, including paying cash for luxurious vacations to the French Riviera with his wife. Detectives got another break when an informant called a tip line and suggested that they investigate men named Farid Allou and Doudou Yahiaoui.

Wiretaps on both men's phones revealed a connection with Djennad and allowed police to hear the men discussing some of the loot, including the thirty-one-carat ring. When the men set a date to divide the cash from the heist, police were ready. On June 21, 2009, they waited for Allou and Yahiaoui to meet and exchange cash, and immediately arrested both men. Djennad was also arrested along with five unnamed accomplices.

THE CASE TODAY

Djennad cooperated fully with investigators and told them about his involvement in deactivating alarms before the first heist. He was sentenced to five years in prison in 2015, with three years of the sentence being suspended. Allou was sentenced to ten years for the heists, and Doudou, whom police had claimed to be the mastermind of the robberies, received fifteen years.

In total, 880 pieces were stolen in both heists. Police recovered several hundred in Doudou's home, but nearly five hundred remain missing to this day.

THE GREEN VAULT HEIST

A heist so valuable the thieves were green with envy.

NOVEMBER 25, 2019 ★ *ANTWERP, BELGIUM*

DESCRIPTION

The Green Vault is a museum in Dresden, located a stone's throw from the River Elbe. It was founded by Augustus the Strong of Poland and Saxony in 1723, and as such claims to be the oldest museum in the world.

The Green Vault's other claim to fame is that it houses Europe's largest treasure collection, though the Vatican probably has more stolen stuff squirreled away in some back room. Still, the museum is incredibly impressive, both in contents and history.

The building dates back to the sixteenth century, when a new wing was ordered to be built onto Dresden Castle by Holy Roman Elector Moritz of Saxony. A block of four rooms of the wing were given a beautiful, molded plaster ceiling and column details, and were painted a rich green color. Moritz decided to use these rooms, with their thick walls and iron gates, to store his treasures

and important documents, it quickly became called "The Green Vault," though the official name was the "Privy Repository."

The Green Vault was used as this private repository throughout the seventeenth century, storing treasures and important documents. In 1723, Augustus the Strong and decided to make the Green Vault publicly viewable. He had elaborate rooms built to house his collections, starting with the Hall of Treasures and Corner Cabinet, which were completed in 1725, according to construction documents. He then began expanding and had eight interconnected rooms built, using Baroque stylings whose beauty was said to match the contents of the room, so he could put his entire collection on display.

Augustus cared about this project a great deal, and used the new rooms to curate and house the treasures, with items grouped together in rooms based on their materials. He had a gold room, an ivory room, a diamond room, and so on. At the end of his reign in 1733, he even made his own crown jewels part of the display, which was unprecedented for the time.

Not much changed for nearly two hundred years, but when World War II seemed imminent, the treasures were moved off-site to Konigstein Fortress. This proved to be a very wise decision, as the building was heavily damaged during the bombing of Dresden in February 1945. Three rooms were completely destroyed, and several others suffered significant damage. At the end of the war, the treasures were taken by the Red Army and moved to the Soviet Union until 1958, when they were returned to Germany. Some of the pieces were displayed in the Albertinum, a different museum in Dresden.

In 2004, construction began on a new Green Vault on the second floor. In 2006, it was completed and the original was restored back to exactly how it originally looked, with nine rooms and an entrance chamber. Both are approximately 2,000 square meters in size.

As to the treasures that the vault housed, there's no way to estimate value accurately; the collection is literally priceless. The star of the museum is the Dresden Green Diamond, a forty-one-carat stone that is green due to natural irradiation,

and naturally internally flawless. Also in the collection were multiple sets of royal jewelry, which included thirty-seven elaborate pieces of jewelry meant to demonstrate the owner's absolute power. In total, there were approximately 4,000 pieces between both of the Green Vaults.

At approximately 4:00 a.m. on November 25, 2019, a power box on the Augustus bridge was set on fire. This fire knocked out electricity to the area and disabled alarm systems and streetlights.

Shortly after, the thieves cut through the metal bars outside the window of the Jewel Room. A CCTV camera unaffected by the power outage showed two thieves in the vault, but police believe there were likely four thieves in total. They crawled through the hole in the bars, only possible because they were small. Once inside, they used axes to smash through the glass displays.

The thieves took three jewelry sets, and the Dresden White Diamond, a forty-nine-carat stone that Augustus loved so much he paid nearly $1 million for it, approximately $100 million in today's money. They also stole an épée sword covered in nine large and seven hundred small diamonds, a brooch containing over 660 gemstones, and an Order of the White Eagle chest star, an award that featured a twenty-carat center diamond and a red ruby Maltese cross. The total value of the haul was over $1 billion.

Once the thieves finished looting, they exited and replaced the window bars to try to avoid detection. They got into an Audi A6 and drove off. The break-in was detected by guards at 4:56 a.m., and over a dozen police cars were sent to the museum. Police set up roadblocks around the area, but by then it was too late, and the museum's proximity to the autobahn entrance made a speedy getaway all too easy.

Later, investigators would find an identical car abandoned in a parking garage and set on fire. In December 2019, police announced that they thought this could be the work of an Arab thief ring operating out of Berlin, but no arrests have been made. They are also investigating four of the security guards to see if they might be involved as inside men. Now they believe that up to seven people are involved in some way.

KNOWN SUSPECTS

This heist has many of the same calling cards that are typical of the world's most notorious gang of jewel thieves, so it's possible that it was pulled off by the Pink Panthers, a group of mostly Serbian and Montenegrin thieves that has as many as two hundred members around the world. One of their MOs is using inside men, and they like to escape via Audis because they feel that they are the most dependable getaway cars.

THE CASE TODAY

So far, none of the stolen goods have been recovered, though in January 2020, an Israeli firm claimed to see some items on the Dark Web.

NOTORIOUS NE'ER-DO-WELLS

The world's premier gang of thieves.

WHO: THE PINK PANTHERS
WHEN: 2003 TO THE PRESENT
WHERE: INTERNATIONAL

CRIMINAL LEGACY

In 2003, two thieves walked into Graff Jewelers' Bond Street location in London. Three minutes later, they walked out the front door with over $30 million in diamonds and precious stones, in the United Kingdom's biggest heist. During the course of the investigation, detectives found a large blue diamond worth $500,000 hidden in a jar of face cream, in what seemed to be an homage to the classic film, *The Return of the Pink Panther*. From that point on, the police would use the nickname "The Pink Panthers" for what would turn out to be the world's premier network of jewel thieves.

Over the next several years, the Pink Panthers would be credited with hundreds of high-profile heists in twenty countries, creating a criminal organization that spanned multiple continents. Founded in Belgrade, Serbia, by Dragan Mikic,

the Pink Panthers quickly grew into a semi-decentralized network of thieves, fences, and general ne'er-do-wells two hundred members strong, though some estimates place the expanded network at closer to eight hundred members. Though there is no formal leader, the Panthers have several cells around the world that work together to pull off heists with regional cell leaders, or break higher-ranking members out of prison. Many members have military backgrounds, and most come from the Balkan region.

Wherever the Panthers strike, though, it is sure to be exciting. In Dubai, they drove two Audi S8s through a shopping mall and smashed through the front door of a jewelry store. In St. Tropez, the thieves were dressed for vacation and made a bold escape on a speedboat. Others use outlandish costumes or beautiful women to act as distractions. While the Pink Panthers prefer not to hurt anyone during robberies, weapons are often used to intimidate victims into compliance. Most heists last only a few minutes, but usually net millions of dollars.

KNOWN HEISTS

Hundreds of heists have been attributed to the Pink Panthers since 2003, including multimillion-dollar jobs in London, Paris, Dubai, Tokyo, Monaco, and the United States. Some of their most famous scores include both Harry Winston heists in Paris, the Comtesse de Vendome necklace heist in Tokyo, and the Carlton Hotel heist in Cannes. The Panthers are also the likeliest suspects in the Kim Kardashian robbery in Paris. It is believed that the Pink Panthers are responsible for the most expensive heists in French and Japanese history.

It's impossible to know exact amounts, but authorities say that the Pink Panthers are responsible for anywhere between $500 million and $1.5 billion in stolen jewels and cash.

THE DINNER SET GANG

Just two best friends living the dream.

1960s–1970s ★ *UNITED STATES*

DESCRIPTION

Just after sunset one night in 1973, at a palatial home in one of Palm Beach's most exclusive neighborhoods, one of the Du Pont family heirs sat down to dinner. Like most dinners for the ultra-wealthy, the meal was several courses and had a number of invited guests. There was an unspoken rule during these dinners that leaving the table was in poor form, so on the mansion's second story, a pair of thieves were free to move about.

With one of the men posted as a lookout, the other moved silently through the master bedroom, and quickly but carefully searched drawers and walk-in closets. When the drawers proved fruitless, he turned his attention to a linen closet and discovered a brown leather satchel hidden among the sheets. Inside were jewels worth over $12,000,000 ($72 million in today's money), including a 17.65 carat pear-shaped pink diamond. The stone was natural, internally flawless,

and was worth just under $2 million ($12 million today) by itself. The thief closed up the satchel, and the pair made their exit through the same window they'd crawled in through. They had just committed the single largest home heist in American history in less than three minutes.

Throughout the 1960s and '70s, the pair of cat burglars, known affectionately as "The Fat Cat Burglars" hit the homes of the mega-wealthy for a string of burglaries that took an estimated $75–$150 million in jewels. Pulling names from the Forbes lists of wealthiest Americans, the duo would look up addresses in the "Who's Who in America'" newsletter, or read multiple-page articles about potential homes in architectural magazines. The burglars robbed many of America's most prominent families, such as the Macys and the Pillsburys. Liberace fell victim to the duo as well.

The thieves rarely deviated from

their modus operandi. After selecting a target, they would perform extensive reconnaissance, learning schedules and observing until an exploitable pattern emerged. While most thieves would wait until the homes were empty, the Dinner Set Gang opted to strike as the victims sat for dinner, preferably with guests. Dinner parties meant that household staff would be preoccupied tending to guests, while the diners would feel compelled to stay seated until every course had been served. Crucially, this also meant that alarms in the home would be turned off.

KNOWN SUSPECTS

While their brazen dinnertime heists eventually earned them the name "The Dinner Set Gang," very few people knew the true identities of the bandits. Peter Salerno and Dominick Latella were best friends from Yonkers, New York, who became brothers-in-law after marrying a pair of identical twin sisters from a Mafia family. Salerno was an incredibly talented burglar with a sixth sense for finding gems and was the protégé of the notorious cat burglar, Frank Bova.

Bova learned to hit houses while people dined during his service as an Army Ranger in World War II, where he was tasked with stealing documents from the homes of German officers. After returning home, Bova found that using his burglar skills was much more lucrative than any other work he could find, and he became known as one of the world's top thieves. When he no longer had the physicality that heists demanded, he began training Salerno and consulted on cases with him, for a fee. Incredibly, Bova was able to retire from a life of crime without ever getting arrested.

Salerno and Latella traveled the country, following the mega rich as they traveled to their winter homes in Florida and back to the northeast for the rest of the year. While Latella stood watch, Salerno scaled the buildings and entered through second-floor windows, usually targeting master bedrooms and nearby closets, allowing himself three minutes to find whatever valuables he could. The duo took any stolen gems to their fence, Wally Gans, in New York City's diamond district on 47th Street. Gans typically paid the men 10 percent of the gems' value, and kept the rest for himself, but this still made Salerno and Latella incredibly wealthy. The pair spent the money nearly as quickly as they made it, buying fancy cars and nice suits, and they kept so much cash on hand that their wives never learned how to write checks.

THE CASE TODAY

The duo retired in the late 1970s without ever getting caught and continued to live the high life throughout the 1980s. However, in 1991, when Salerno's wife, Gloria, was diagnosed with cancer, medical bills quickly drained his savings. Salerno and Latella decided to pay for Gloria's treatment the best way they knew how and started robbing homes again. Rather than conducting extensive recon like they'd done in the 1960s, the duo instead opted for speed, performing over forty heists in the span of a few months.

On January 21, 1992, they targeted a home in Westport, Connecticut. As Latella watched the residents sit for dinner, Salerno tried to enter the second-story window—but he made a loud noise on the way in. Latella saw one of the residents look up at the sound and whistled to alert Salerno. Salerno managed to exit the house before police arrived, but their getaway driver had been scared off, so the two men were forced to escape on foot. Latella and Salerno evaded the officers at first, but when police brought in dogs to assist, the men were both found hiding in a pile of leaves and arrested.

Both men were charged with burglary for the Westport case and several of their previous heists, and sentenced to prison. Peter Salerno was released from prison in December 2008, and he currently lives in Florida with Gloria. Dominick Latella also moved to Florida following his release from prison. He passed away on September 6, 2017.

★ ★ ★

TWIN IT TO WIN IT

WHO: GERMAN HEIST TWINS ★ WHEN: JANUARY 2009 ★ WHERE: BERLIN, GERMANY

IN JANUARY 2009, THREE THIEVES PULLED OFF A MISSION: IMPOSSIBLE—STYLE HEIST AT THE UPSCALE BERLIN DEPARTMENT STORE KAUFHAUS DES WESTENS. RAPPELLING DOWN ROPES FROM THE BUILDING'S SKYLIGHTS, THE THIEVES WERE ABLE TO STEAL NEARLY $7 MILLION IN JEWELRY BEFORE MAKING THEIR ESCAPE VIA A ROPE LADDER. THOUGH THE THIEVES WERE CAREFUL, ONE OF THEM ACCIDENTALLY LEFT BEHIND A LATEX GLOVE THAT CONTAINED THEIR SWEAT.

AUTHORITIES WERE ABLE TO PULL DNA FROM THE GLOVE AND THE RESULTS YIELDED NOT ONE, BUT TWO SUSPECTS. IDENTICAL TWIN BROTHERS HASSAN O. AND ABBAS O. (GERMAN LAW PREVENTED THE RELEASE OF THEIR FULL NAMES) WERE ARRESTED BY POLICE ON FEBRUARY 11, 2009, BUT BECAUSE POLICE WERE UNABLE TO CONCLUSIVELY DETERMINE WHICH OF THE TWINS HAD BEEN INVOLVED IN THE HEIST, CHARGES AGAINST BOTH BROTHERS WERE DROPPED, AND THEY WERE SET FREE. NOBODY ELSE HAS BEEN CHARGED.

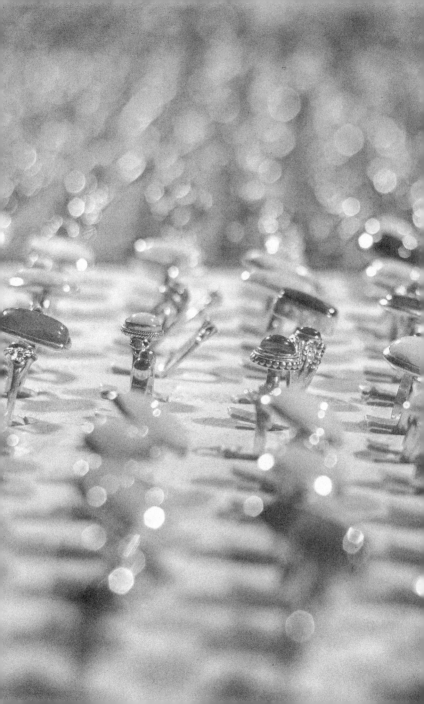

CHAPTER 5
CYBER HEISTS

They don't make heists like they used to. Back in the day, you got dressed up to go rob a bank; now these thieves are doing it in their pajamas. Whatever they're wearing, cybercriminals pose an increasingly large threat every day, as they steal everything from money to identities. As the world becomes increasingly more digital, the craftiest thieves are finding ways to expand their operations into cyberspace and pull off bigger heists than ever, without the hassle of finding a fence. Con men are also embracing the digital age and putting new spins on classic scams.

THE CONSTABLE CYBER HEIST

Why steal a painting when you can just take the money?

DESCRIPTION

A View of Hampstead Heath: Child's Hill, Harrow in the Distance was painted by John Constable in 1824, and, as the name implies, it is a beautiful landscape painting of London parks and countryside, and features cattle and a horse-drawn carriage. It's one of several paintings that Constable made overlooking Hampstead Heath.

Constable, an English painter, is referred to as a revolutionary of landscapes now, but in his own lifetime he wasn't very financially successful. This particular painting was sold among mostly private collections but did spend twenty-three years on loan to the Whitworth Gallery in London. In 2018, it was acquired by art dealer Simon Dickinson and was promptly displayed at the European Fine Art Fair.

The painting had lots of interested buyers, but none were as interested as Arnoud Odding, who was the director of the Rijksmuseum Twenthe, a Dutch art museum in Enschede that boasts a collection of over 10,000 pieces. The museum was missing a work by Constable, and this was Odding's chance to finally get one.

Odding didn't have enough money to buy the painting outright, but he asked if he could put the painting on display in his museum to help raise the funds and then complete the sale. Dickinson agreed to these terms and a sale price of £2.4 million (just over $3 million).

The museum received the painting and tested the work to ensure its authenticity. It then put the work on display and raised the money through a combination of private donors and a government arts grant. With the money raised, Odding and Dickinson scheduled a date for the payment via wire transfer. Dickinson provided his bank account routing information, and Odding prepared to send the money.

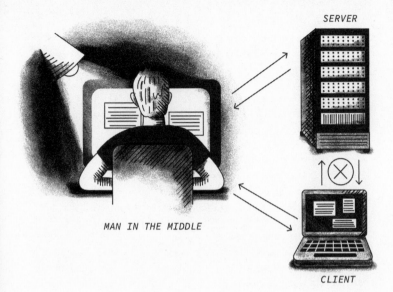

SERVER

MAN IN THE MIDDLE

CLIENT

On the day of the transfer, Odding got an email from the Simon C. Dickinson LTD Gallery with updated routing info for the payment. Odding entered the new account numbers and sent the payment, but Dickinson never received the money. When Dickinson called to ask about his payment, Odding replied that he had wired the money to the new account numbers like Dickinson asked. When the wire transfer was analyzed by the banks, they discovered that the money was sent to an account in Hong Kong and vanished without a trace immediately after the transfer completed.

KNOWN SUSPECTS

While authorities are still working to determine exactly how the cyberattack happened and who did it, there are three scenarios that are most likely. First, the simplest option is that the thief set up a fake email address to send the banking details for an offshore account they set up. This scenario doesn't seem to be likely because the hacker had access to the existing email chain.

Second, there is a possibility that someone hacked Dickinson's legitimate email address. This is pretty simple to do with a phishing attack, the act of sending an email with a malicious link or file, so that you can get a foothold in somebody's network. For example, a hacker could send an email with a link to a piece of malware that logs the victim's keystrokes. If the victim clicked that link, the hacker would be able to see everything that the victim typed and would get access to passwords, etc. This would allow the attacker to sign into the victims' legitimate email address to send emails with updated routing information without raising suspicions. If the hacker was particularly savvy, they could also delete the sent emails so that the Dickinson Gallery would have no record of the change. This is probably the smartest way to pull off this kind of heist, especially with a target like Dickinson's gallery that sells lots of high-value items. This scam could potentially happen again and again.

Third, there is a scenario called a "Man in the Middle Attack." Like the name implies, in this situation, the hacker places themselves between the two parties, intercepting their emails and then forwarding them to each party after reading or modifying the messages. This kind of attack will typically have a higher degree of difficulty and might again point to having inside help due to the timing.

THE CASE TODAY

The hack kicked off an intense legal battle between the Dickinson Gallery and the museum, with both parties claiming that they should have custody of the painting. Both sides make compelling arguments, but until this is settled in the courts, the painting is stillin the possession of the museum but is not on display. Currently, police have not identified any suspects in the hack.

NOTORIOUS NE'ER-DO-WELLS

All in The Scamily

WHO: SCAMMERS
WHEN: 1800–PRESENT
WHERE: GLOBAL

The Nigerian Prince Scam is a modern variation of an Advance Fee Scam, which is itself a modernized version of the Spanish Prisoner Scam. As the name implies, the Advance Fee Scam consists of somebody contacting a potential victim and telling them that they have discovered a huge sum of money that they cannot access alone. However, with a bit of financial assistance from the victim and a bit of derring-do on the prince's part, the vast fortune can be had and split between both parties, usually to the tune of 10 to 40 percent.

The Spanish Prisoner Scam was basically the same thing, but usually involved somebody reaching out to a victim stating that a wealthy Spanish royal has been imprisoned but can't reveal their identity to their captors without being killed. Therefore, they need to raise enough money to bribe the guards for the prisoner's release, and in exchange they'll provide

money and the hand of a beautiful female relative to marry off to the person who paid the bail.

The most common variation of the modern Advance Fee Scam is an exiled prince trying to reclaim his family fortune or move it out of the country due to rising tensions, but again there are countless variations of this.

Most of the time, these scams are done in volume, meaning they send emails out to fifty million people asking for smaller sums of money, sometimes a few hundred bucks, sometimes a few thousand, or even tens of thousands, but because they're going out to so many people, these scams are insanely lucrative. If half a percent of that fifty million gets tricked into sending $1,000, that's 250,000 people and $250 million! Interpol estimates that most Nigerian Prince email scammers steal an average of $700,000 annually.

THE NIGERIAN AIRPORT SCAM

Everyone's heard of the Nigerian Prince Scam, but one man took it to a whole new level.

1995–1997 ★ ABUJA, NIGERIA

DESCRIPTION

In 1995, Nelson Sakaguchi, a manager at Banco Noroeste in Brazil, saw an email from the governor of the Central Bank of Nigeria, Paul Ogwuma, asking for funds to help approve and construct a new airport in Ajuba. As the manager of a large bank, Sakaguchi was used to seeing big deals go through, but at $242 million, this deal was bigger than most. Further down in the message, Sakaguchi saw that he'd be eligible for a 10 percent commission; that much money would change his life forever.

Of course, Sakaguchi wasn't going to just hand the money over right away. He requested more details, and soon he was looking at proposal documents, financial tables, construction estimates, and, as this project was not ready to go public, there were some nondisclosure agreements as well.

Everything seemed to be in order.

Ogwuma told him that the approval process might take years, and that he'd be updated on any developments as they came. Sakaguchi was convinced. He double checked the paperwork, thought about the $24 million he stood to make, and approved the loan and wired $191 million to be held in escrow in several accounts in the Cayman Islands.

Of course, there was no airport. Sakaguchi was the unsuspecting victim of the third-largest financial scam in history, despite his extensive banking experience. Unfortunately for Sakaguchi, the scammer had even deeper ties to banking.

KNOWN SUSPECTS

Emmanuel Nwude worked as the director of the Union Bank of Nigeria, which gave him access to classified information, and unmatched familiarity with the banking system. In 1995, Nwude impersonated the governor of the Central Bank of Nigeria, Paul Ogwuma, and reached out to Sakaguchi.

Having seen the requisite paperwork for similar deals that he'd brokered legitimately as a bank director, Nwude and a few unnamed accomplices provided copies of official-looking paperwork to help legitimize the deal. After the money had been sent, Nwude would provide periodic updates about the approval process, citing delays but assuring Sakaguchi that the plan would still go through eventually.

It's impossible to know how long Nwude would have been able to keep this ruse going, but in 1997, Banco Noroeste was acquired by Spanish banking giant Santander. While performing their due diligence, Santander discovered that a whole 40 percent of Banco Noroeste's capital was unaccounted for and had been wired to the Caymans. After interest, the amount was discovered to be $330 million.

THE CASE TODAY

Santander launched an investigation immediately, but it took them over seven years to arrest Nwude and his accomplices. In 2004, they were taken before the Abuja high court and charged with eighty-six counts of fraudulent advance fees and fifteen counts of bribery. Almost immediately, Nwude tried to bribe these officials as well. The case was eventually dismissed by a judge who claimed that they lacked jurisdiction for a crime that didn't occur in Abuja.

The defendants were immediately arrested when they left the courthouse and a new trial began in Lagos. After trying to bribe this judge as well, the court had to be evacuated for a bomb scare. Eventually, the prosecution was able to get Sakaguchi to testify directly, and, soon after, all of the defendants pled guilty in exchange for lighter sentences.

Nwude was sentenced to twenty-five years in prison, fined $10 million dollars, and all of his assets were seized. Ultimately, Nwude would serve only a year of his sentence, and was released in 2006. Upon his release, he filed a lawsuit to reclaim some assets he claimed he'd had before he committed the crimes. So far, he's recovered at least $50 million.

After his release, he was named president-general (basically a mayor) of Ugbene town, but in 2016, he was arrested again for being the suspected ringleader in a terrorist attack against the town of Ukpo, where a mob of over two hundred people showed up and a security guard was killed. Nwude was charged with murder and terrorism and is currently out on bail serving as president-general of Ugbene.

ICELANDIC BITCOIN HEIST

Why steal money when you can just make it instead?

JANUARY 16, 2018 ★ *ICELAND*

DESCRIPTION

On the night of December 5, 2017, a small team of thieves pulled up to the Algrim Consulting data center in Asbru, Iceland. They searched the compound for their target and before long, they saw that one of the buildings had an open window, which would normally have been unusual given that it was the dead of winter in Iceland.

This wasn't an ordinary data center though; it was a bitcoin mine. Unlike standard mines, there was no digging beneath the earth happening here; everything was digital. Instead of pulling bitcoins from the ground, miners earned the cryptocurrency by completing increasingly complex math problems called blockchain blocks. Whoever solved the problems first earned one bitcoin for their troubles, setting off a digital arms race for miners trying to get the biggest and fastest computers. To accomplish this, miners would often create supercomputers made of small but incredibly powerful computers known as Asics.

These computers were highly specialized—purpose-built for solving enormous equations as quickly as possible—and this computing power grew exponentially when several machines were connected together. That much computing power comes at a cost, though. Bitcoin mining computers used a lot of electricity and tend to run very hot, often at the risk of overheating.

Because of this, Iceland was perhaps the most ideal location on the planet to run a bitcoin mine. It offered extremely cheap electricity thanks to the abundant geothermal power supplies, and its frigid temperatures acted as a natural cooling system for the computers, allowing them to run for extended periods of time without performance issues. Plus, Iceland had a very low crime rate.

Due to the anonymous nature of bitcoin, these computers were ideal targets for thieves. The computers themselves were very valuable, but if you used the computers to create a mine of your own, you could essentially just print money.

Once the thieves spotted the open windows, they looked for the best way into the building and quickly found a ladder next to the open window. They climbed in and quickly disconnected the mining computers, loading them into their van. They took 104 computers in total, plus a few graphics cards, which could also be used in standard PCs to compute blockchain blocks. Once everything was loaded up, the men drove off, trying to avoid suspicion. Over a hundred Asics was a great start for a mine, but they were just getting started.

A few days later, one of the thieves' friends, an electrician, told him about another data center that just requested a massive increase in their electrical needs. Another mine was popping up,

and the thieves would be ready.

Just after 2:00 a.m. on December 15, the team of thieves drove a van up to a lonely warehouse in Borgarnes, Iceland about an hour north of Reykjavik. After breaking into the three-story building, owned by a tech firm called AVK, they found another stash of miners. These computers hadn't been there long, only a few days. In fact, they were so new that they hadn't even been plugged in yet.

The thieves moved quickly. They loaded up all twenty-eight computers, each about the size of a loaf of bread, and any power supplies, graphics cards, or other peripherals into the van and drove off. They took the shortest way home again, this time via the Whale Fjord Tunnel. Unbeknownst to them, a security camera at the tunnel entrance captured a photo of the van and the passengers.

KNOWN SUSPECTS

When police investigated the break-in at the AVK data center, they pulled up the CCTV footage from the tunnel, matched it with a nearby hardware store's security camera footage showing the same vehicle, and ran the plates for the van, which had recently been purchased by Matthais Karlsson.

Police arrested Karlsson and Sindri Thor Stefansson, the suspected ringleader, and brought them in for questioning. After three days of interviews, where the men denied having any part in the heist, police had no choice but to release them due to lack of evidence, though they

did discover that Stefansson had an extensive criminal history with over two hundred charges for petty theft and other crimes.

Karlsson's arrest cost him his job as a day care teacher, and he was desperate for money to make ends meet. Stefansson had told him that he had another job coming up and that he'd find Karlsson a part in the heist. Stefansson had a new target in mind that would be big enough to make them all very rich for a very long time. Another, bigger mine had been started up at the Advania Data Center, housed on a formal naval base just outside Reykjavik, but this mine had more advanced security.

Stefansson and his childhood best friend Hafthor Hylnsson, a.k.a. Haffi the Pink, decided to get an inside man. After identifying a security guard named Ivar Gylfason, Stefansson had a relative of Ivar's ex-girlfriend call him. She owed Haffi some money, and Ivar was threatened into providing details about the security coverage at the warehouse. Reluctantly, Ivar agreed, and held two meetings with Stefansson where he provided answers to the questions the thieves had.

On the night of January 16, 2018, it was time to act. Stefansson knew that there would only be one guard that night and knew his patrol schedule. By a stroke of luck, the guard fell ill with stomach issues and abandoned his post to go home. Stefansson texted Haffi, who was directing the team from Spain, and told him that it was time to head in. By a second stroke of luck, the motion detectors at the data center were not hooked up to the alarms; the thieves would have free range of motion in the data center.

Stefansson sent another text to Karlsson and his brother, Petur, and the two men pulled their van up to the Advania Data Center. Covering their faces with scarves, they filled their van with mining computers, 225 of them. The hardware alone was worth over half a million dollars. After the van was loaded up, Karlsson and his brother drove off. The team had just pulled off the largest heist in Iceland's history.

Police moved quickly, hoping to make an example of the robbers and to make it known that Iceland was still a safe place to mine bitcoin. Within two weeks, they'd identified Gylfason as the inside man and arrested him. The brothers Karlsson were also arrested at about the same time.

Stefansson had planned on fleeing to Spain with his wife and children, but was arrested at his in-laws' home while packing his family's belongings onto a pallet. Police found a hand-drawn map of the Advania facility in his pants pocket. His phone and computer were seized and sent to Denmark for analysis. Despite the evidence, Stefansson pleaded not guilty in court. During the trial it was revealed that his phone still contained text messages to the crew during the heists.

THE CASE TODAY

While awaiting sentencing, Stefansson escaped from jail and hitchhiked to the airport where he boarded a plane bound for Sweden. Coincidentally, he was on the same flight as Iceland's prime minister. After reaching Sweden, Stefansson fled to Denmark, where he met with Haffi and another friend named Viktor "The Cutie" Jonasson, and stupidly posted a selfie that he hashtagged with "#TeamSindri." Within hours, he was arrested again and extradited to Iceland.

Once the trial began, Stefansson pleaded guilty to two of the burglaries and was sentenced to four-and-a-half years. Matthias Karlsson was sentenced to two-and-a-half years and his brother, Petur, received eighteen months for his role in the Advania heist. Haffi, Viktor, and the security guard Ivar were handed sentences ranging from fifteen to twenty months. The men were also ordered to pay police over $115,000 in legal fees incurred during the investigation. With the exception of Ivar Gylafson, all of the thieves have appealed their convictions, and Icelandic law states that they are free until their conviction appeals are resolved.

The bitcoin mining computers have never been recovered. When asked about them in a recent interview, Stefansson quipped that "maybe the computers have been running the whole time. Maybe I know where they are. Maybe I do, and maybe I don't."

THE BANGLADESHI BANK HEIST

Hackers pulled off one of the biggest bank robberies in history, without stepping foot into the bank.

FEBRUARY 4, 2016 ★ *BANGLADESH*

DESCRIPTION

On February 4, 2016, the central bank of Bangladesh sent out thirty-five wire transfer requests via the global banking network SWIFT. The requests totaled nearly $1 billion and sought to move funds from Bangladesh Bank's holdings at the Federal Reserve Bank of New York (FRBNY) to thirty-five accounts around the world, including four in the Philippines and one in Sri Lanka. There was only one problem, though; Bangladesh Bank didn't make those SWIFT requests, hackers did.

Like a traditional bank heist, this hack took years of preparation. First, the hackers needed to pick a target. Whereas a traditional brick-and-mortar bank robbery might not yield much more than $100,000 on a good day, a country's central bank would likely contain billions. The thieves now needed to find a country that had a growing economy but

also had a weaker communications infrastructure. Eventually, they picked Bangladesh.

Next, the hackers needed to scout things out, so they sent out phishing emails. They created sophisticated malware and embedded it into a PDF file of a fake resume that they emailed to several Bangladesh Bank employees. At least three of the employees downloaded the resume, which automatically began installing malicious code onto their machines. While this malware did not provide the hackers with access to the bank's entire network, it did allow them to monitor the day-to-day operations of the users they'd phished. From there, employees were able to identify which users might have access to critical networks or have elevated privilege to perform functions like approving transfers. The hackers also discovered who had access to the SWIFT terminal.

SWIFT is a massive network of banks that spans over 11,000 financial institutions in more than two hundred countries and territories. Only approved banks are eligible to join the network, but once banks join, they are able to submit and receive money transfers between other SWIFT member banks in a standardized and reliable manner. Requests are made using specialized identification codes that indicate the names of the banks involved and the country of origin of those banks. Even within the banks themselves, access to SWIFT is limited to only essential staff and requires secure credentials to access.

After performing months of online reconnaissance and lateral movement through the bank's networks, the hackers were able to obtain the necessary SWIFT credentials, and began observing how the bank made their transfers and which accounts contained the most funds. They learned that Bangladesh Bank had approximately $1 billion kept in their account at the Federal Reserve Bank of NY, and that several smaller transfers were less scrutinized than a single large withdrawal. The thieves began setting up bank accounts all over the world, each opened with $500 deposits and then essentially abandoned.

After months of observation, they learned that when the Bangladesh Bank made a transfer request, the network automatically sent a copy of the request to an HP printer which produced a physical copy of the request and would be reviewed by one of the managers at the bank, who could decline transactions that were not approved. If everything seemed OK, the bank where the money was being held would perform a transfer from the client's account to the destination account, but only after performing their own review of the request. Cleverly, the hackers created another piece of malware targeted at Bangladesh Bank's SWIFT printer that caused the machine to print only blank pages before deleting the print history. With that work done, it was time to pick a date.

In a stroke of utter genius, the thieves planned to commit their hack on Thursday, February 4, 2016, just after closing hours at Bangladesh Bank. After logging into the Bangladesh Bank's SWIFT terminal, the hackers sent out thirty-five transfer requests from the bank's FRBNY account to the bank accounts around the world they'd created nearly a year earlier. Because Bangladesh observes the weekend on Friday and Saturday, nobody from that bank would be in to see the requests until Sunday, at which time FRBNY would be closed for their weekend. That weekend also coincided with the Lunar New Year, so banks across Asia would be closed on Monday as well, allowing the thieves to have up to five days where the banks could not communicate with each other.

While thirty of the requests were flagged by various banks for increased scrutiny, five of the requests, worth $101 million, went through and money was sent to four accounts at RCBC banks in the Philippines and one account in Sri Lanka. The Sri Lanka request was promptly refunded, though, when bankers at a German intermediary bank noticed a suspicious spelling error and routed the $20 million back to Bangladesh Bank. The money that went to the accounts in the Philippines, however, was deposited without issue and was forwarded to accounts at two large casinos.

Once the money, $81 million in total, hit the casino bank accounts, a group of Chinese nationals requested junket rooms, reserved for the largest whales, to gamble in. The men played baccarat for several hours with the stolen money, and when they'd played long enough to avoid suspicion, they exchanged their chips for clean cash that could not be tied to the heist and disappeared.

KNOWN SUSPECTS

Investigations at Bangladesh Bank, FRBNY, and other banks around the world were immediately opened and soon revealed that the attack was too sophisticated to have been the work of a traditional group of hackers. The skills and resources needed to perform a heist against the SWIFT platform itself had only been seen before in hacks like the one that targeted Sony. Before long, investigators and security researchers around the world found enough evidence to formally implicate the North Korean government as the perpetrators, specifically attributing the attack to a branch of North Korea's Lazarus Group hacking collective known as the BeagleBoyz.

THE CASE TODAY

Due to extradition laws and geo-politics, no arrests of North Korean hackers related to the crime have been made, but international sanctions were increased against North Korea. A former manager at RCBC bank in the Philippines was charged and convicted of money laundering for facilitating the transfers to the casinos and was sentenced to four to seven years of prison.

The Bangladesh Bank heist did ultimately see $81 million vanish, but did inspire massive security overhauls at banks around the world and internally at SWIFT. International anti-money laundering groups have also pledged to implement steps to prevent such a heist from happening again, though it's only a matter of time before attackers figure out a way around these new measures.

NOTORIOUS NE'ER-DO-WELLS

Making money however possible.

WHO: THE LAZARUS GROUP
WHEN: CIRCA 2009–PRESENT
WHERE: DEMOCRATIC PEOPLE'S REPUBLIC OF KOREA (NORTH KOREA)

On November 24, 2014, news broke that Sony Pictures had been the victim of a massive data breach. Over the next several weeks, a group calling themselves "The Guardians of Peace" began leaking private emails between studio executives, actor pay information, and even films that had not been released. The hack was a devastating blow to Sony and Hollywood as a whole and seemed to be retaliation for a movie Sony had produced titled *The Interview*, where James Franco and Seth Rogen travel to North Korea and are asked to assassinate President Kim Jong Un by the CIA. While no money was directly stolen from Sony, the hack cost the company billions of dollars.

In 2017, the world would be held hostage by the WannaCry ransomware attacks. WannaCry infected at least 300,000 computers worldwide, encrypting or deleting the computers'

data and telling users that the data could only be recovered if a ransom was paid in bitcoin. Sadly, when users paid the hackers' ransom, the hackers more often than not provided fake decryption codes or vanished completely.

These two attacks may seem unrelated, but both were conclusively attributed to hackers in North Korea. While North Korea has a reputation for lagging behind the rest of the world technologically, the country is actually home to one of the world's most sophisticated hacking collectives, known to security experts as Lazarus Group. Thought to be founded in 2009, Lazarus Group has directly or indirectly been involved in many of the world's most terrifying cyberattacks, including the attempted billion-dollar hack of the Bangladesh Bank and multiple cryptocurrency-based attacks in 2017.

By leveraging the resources available to a nation-state and the autonomy to ignore extradition laws, Lazarus Group has been able to conduct increasingly sophisticated and lucrative hacks, including several in 2020 that saw Lazarus Group members pretending to be doctors and pharmaceutical executives in order to effectively spread ransomware that was disguised as information about the COVID-19 pandemic. Lazarus Group was also able to leverage the security gaps that appeared when the pandemic shutdowns almost overnight forced companies to work remotely. Each of these cyberattacks has netted the North Korean government hundreds of millions of dollars in ransoms or full-blown heists.

COUNTERFEITING OPERATIONS

Cybercrime, however, is not the only illicit activity that the North Korean government participates in. North Korea is currently the world's second-leading producer of United States currency, thanks to its extraordinarily sophisticated counterfeiting operations. North Korea's status as a nation-state allows it access to buy the same paper blends and printers that other countries use to create their own currencies, and they have used that access to print hundreds of millions of dollars in counterfeit money that is visually indistinguishable from authentic cash printed by the United States Treasury. North Korean bills are of such high quality that the Secret Service has used the name "Super Dollars" for the North Korean counterfeits.

CHAPTER 6
THEY STOLE WHAT?

Remember watching Carmen Sandiego sneaking
around the world to steal Niagara Falls and
thinking, "There's no way someone could steal
a river!"? Well, you might be surprised by this
chapter. Whether you're after sunken treasure or
toilet paper, these thieves prove that you can steal
anything if you get creative enough. Sometimes life
is about knowing what you want and taking it, even
if what you want is really weird.

THE ORIGINAL ITALIAN JOB

Two of history's greatest minds try to pull off the impossible.

EARLY SIXTEENTH CENTURY ★ *FLORENCE, ITALY*

DESCRIPTION

Italy in the early 1500s had recovered from the collapse of the Roman Empire and was essentially a collection of city-states. These city-states modeled themselves after the Roman Republic, and each city-state was traditionally ruled by that city's most powerful and wealthy family.

Milan had the Sforza family, Florence had the Medicis, and these families were each trying to make their cities the cultural centers of the world. They raced to hire artists like Michelangelo, Donatello, Bernini, and others to create masterpieces for them, and hired engineers, builders, and generals to make their cities the best. It was probably the closest thing in history to a real-life game of *Civilization 5*. Each tried to acquire more money, create more wonders, and destroy the competition, which was essentially every other city.

This brings us to Florence. The city is located smack in the middle of

Italy, kind of in the kneecap of the boot. It's far from either coast, but still prosperous. Florence was one of the most powerful city-states in all of Italy, mostly due to the Medici family, whose banking brought them tremendous wealth and influence. They were virtually at war with Pisa, their main rival and neighbor along the River Arno.

The Florentine court was trying to find more ways to increase their wealth and standing while also sticking it to Pisa, and they reached out to the closest thing Italy had to Littlefinger, a man named Niccolò Machiavelli, who was serving in the Florentine court at the time.

Machiavelli went to see the Borgias, who were one of the most powerful families in Italy. They were originally from Spain but moved to Italy because of potential power of controlling the papacy. Indeed, two members of the Borgia family were

eventually elected pope. While Machiavelli was speaking to the Borgias, he also met Leonardo da Vinci, who was residing in their court and had just finished building siege engines for the Sforzas in Milan.

Leonardo da Vinci didn't start out by marketing himself as an artist; he first came into the courts of wealthy Italian families by promoting his other skills, such as bridge building, weapons design, and general combat engineering. He didn't emphasize his artistic skills, stating simply that he could paint or draw "as well as any other." He started out as Renaissance-era Tony Stark and only then became the world's greatest artist.

So, Italy's greatest political mind met with Italy's greatest creative mind. Some wine was probably shared, and they came up with a plan that would dramatically increase Florence's wealth, while striking a significant blow to Pisa, all without shedding blood. They were going to steal the River Arno.

Stealing the Arno, or more accurately rerouting it, would allow Florence to irrigate more crops and sell the excess water, and da Vinci even planned a series of canals that would allow ships to sail directly from the Mediterranean to Florence. It's like building a harbor in Kansas.

Machiavelli and da Vinci set up detailed plans that involved tunneling through whole mountains, moving millions of tons of earth, and digging several sets of canals to reroute the river during construction. They envisioned a workforce of over 50,000 men, and once the plans were finalized, Machiavelli took them back to Florence to set things in motion.

They hired an engineer named Columbino and the work began, but the project ended up taking far longer than expected, partly due to the nature of construction projects and partly due to Pisans launching repeated attacks on the work crews. Columbino was pressured to get the job done faster, so he decided to make a few changes to the schematics. Leonardo da Vinci started designing machinery to help with the construction, but none of it was ever built.

Da Vinci had set out plans to dig a massive single trench, measuring eighty feet wide and thirty feet deep, and spanning over a mile long to divert the water away from another construction site. But Columbino instead opted to dig two smaller, shallower trenches (one sixty feet wide by fourteen feet deep, and the second forty by fourteen feet), operating under the assumption that the river would end up eroding them into the larger trench.

When the time came to let the river flow into the trenches, the Arno's water flow completely destroyed both trenches almost immediately. After the trenches were destroyed, the Arno ran pretty much along the same route that it always had and the plans for stealing the river were abandoned, thus ending one of the most ambitious buddy heists ever attempted. It just goes to show you that when the world's smartest person tells you how to do something, you should probably listen.

THE CASE TODAY

Eventually, Pisa and Florence did make peace without having to divert any rivers. Leonardo da Vinci went on to become one of history's most renowned artists. In fact, the Arno River serves as the background for the *Mona Lisa*.

THE GOLDEN BOOS

There are no small heists, only small heisters.

EIGHTEENTH CENTURY ★ *LIECHTENSTEIN*

DESCRIPTION

In Liechtenstein, late one night in 1780, a gorgeous woman with long, auburn hair walked through the front door of a roadside inn. Over her shoulder, she carried a large wooden chest, which she let down with a thud as she sat at the tavern bar. After a pint or two and some friendly conversation with the innkeeper, she inquired about a room for the night. She explained that she had been traveling for several days to go back to her family after her husband's untimely death, and that she had packed her most precious belongings in the chest.

Before turning in for the night, she asked the innkeeper if she could store the chest in the inn's most secure room, as it was too valuable to be left overnight in a standard room. The innkeeper, charmed by her story and her beauty, offered to keep the chest in the same locked room where he kept his own valuables. Relieved at the kind offer, the woman thanked him, finished her drink, and went up to her bedroom, once her trunk was safely locked away.

The next morning, the innkeeper woke up and discovered that the woman was gone. When he went downstairs to check on the chest, he found that it too was missing, along with all of the other valuables that had been locked in the room. Unbeknownst to the innkeeper, the chest hadn't contained treasures at all. Instead, a little person waited inside the chest until everybody in the inn was asleep and then emerged and stole any valuables that were locked in the room with him. Once all of the loot was in the chest, he and the woman escaped into the night.

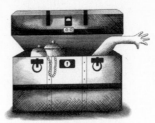

KNOWN SUSPECTS

While that story might sound like a farfetched traveler's tale, it is actually well documented in history. Barbara Erni performed this crime on at least seventeen occasions all over the Alpine region of Europe.

Erni was born to homeless parents on February 15, 1743, in the town of Feldkirch, Austria, near the borders of Switzerland and Liechtenstein. She grew up to be a beautiful woman whose bright orange hair earned her the nickname "The Golden Boos." Because "boos" is Dutch for "angry" or "wicked," her nickname likely meant something like "the wicked redhead." Not much is known about her early life, but historical records show that at the age of thirty-six in 1779 she married a man named Tiroler Franz. Franz was a known criminal himself with a penchant for confidence tricks, and it is likely that he and Barbara planned this scheme together.

Barbara spent several years traveling across Europe and performing this scam as often as she could; she eventually became an incredibly wealthy woman. In fact, her wealth would lead to her undoing when people began to realize that a woman as wealthy as Erni should be staying in nicer accommodations than roadside inns.

THE CASE TODAY

In May 1784, near the town of Eschen, Liechtenstein, Barbara and her still unnamed accomplice were caught in the act of robbing an inn. After being taken to jail, Barbara confessed to performing seventeen robberies in the hopes that her confession would lead to a more lenient sentence. Unfortunately for Barbara, revealing the scale of her crimes had the opposite effect; it angered the people of Liechtenstein so badly that they demanded that she and her accomplice both be executed, which was so rare at the time that Liechtenstein had to bring in an executioner from outside the country.

Barbara Erni and her accomplice were beheaded on February 26, 1785. Barbara actually holds the distinction of being the last person to be executed in Liechtenstein, as capital punishment was abolished two hundred years later in 1987.

ONE OF THE WORST HEISTS OF ALL TIME

This thief put the ID in "Idiot."

WHO: A BONEHEAD IN BRISTOL
WHEN: AUGUST 13, 2008
WHERE: BRISTOL, UNITED KINGDOM

DESCRIPTION

After a rash of recent car break-ins that targeted high-tech GPS units, police in Bristol decided to set up a bait car in order to lure in thieves. An old Peugeot 106 was outfitted with multiple hidden cameras and then moved into a parking garage that had been the site of several recent burglaries.

Within hours, the bait car attracted a thief, who immediately spotted the car's navigation system and tried to open the door with a screwdriver. When the doors couldn't be unlocked or pried open, the thief grew frustrated and broke into the car the old-fashioned way, by smashing the window. Once the window was gone, the burglar crawled into the passenger's seat and removed the navigation unit from the car's dashboard. Minutes later, the thief had successfully removed the GPS, exited the car with his stolen goods, and gone home.

KNOWN SUSPECTS

On September 4, Bristol police arrived at the home of Aaron Evans and placed him under arrest for the theft. Evans, who had an extensive criminal record for previous burglaries, was clearly caught on the hidden cameras in the car, making the case a slam dunk for prosecutors. Incredibly, the video was even more useful for the detectives charged with finding him. In fact, the only reason it took police three weeks to arrest him was because they hadn't watched the footage until the day they made the arrest.

WHAT WENT WRONG

When police finally watched the footage of Evans climbing into the car, they noticed an enormous tattoo on the side of the thief's neck, showing his name and complete birthday. Police ran a quick search of both, which pulled up a previous mug shot and Evans's home address. They went on to make the easiest arrest of the day.

THE GREAT CANADIAN MAPLE SYRUP HEIST

This is a stick-up!

2011–2012 ★ *QUEBEC, CANADA*

DESCRIPTION

In Quebec, almost all maple syrup is regulated by FPAQ, or the Federation of Maple Syrup Producers in Quebec. Quebec provides about 70 percent of the world's maple syrup, and FPAQ can force producers to meet a quota each year for how much syrup they can sell. Anything produced that goes over the quota gets put into reserve storage, called the International Strategic Reserve.

These quotas allow FPAQ to keep a steady supply of syrup flowing to the world, and the reserves help ensure that even during years with less than great harvests, they are always in control of the supply and demand of syrup. This actually works extremely well and as a result, a barrel of syrup is worth about fifty times more than a barrel of crude oil on average.

Typically, FPAQ keeps these syrup reserves stored in labeled white fifty-five-gallon barrels weighing approximately six hundred pounds. These barrels are stored across Quebec using space rented in various barns and warehouses, and FPAC agents conduct annual inspections of the warehouses to ensure their inventory is in line with expectations. While these checks worked well for accountability, they left much to be desired from a security perspective.

Over the period of several months between 2011 and 2012, a group of thieves began trucking syrup barrels from a warehouse in Saint-Louis-de-Blandford to a processing plant known as a "sugar shack," where they siphoned the syrup into unmarked barrels and refilled the FPAQ barrels with water. The water barrels were then taken back to the warehouse where they could be counted during the inventory. The stolen syrup was then broken down into small batches and sold to black-market distributors.

Demand for the black-market syrup grew quickly, and eventually the thieves began siphoning it off without refilling the barrels with water, in order to move more quickly. In July 2012, a FPAQ auditor arrived at the warehouse to begin the annual inventory, but when he tried to climb on one of the barrels, it toppled over, empty. After discovering several other barrels in the immediate area were also empty, FPAQ conducted a full inventory of all of the warehouse's barrels. They discovered that a total of 9,571 barrels of syrup had been stolen, worth a staggering $18 million Canadian.

KNOWN SUSPECTS

Due to the nature of the crime, authorities were quickly able to determine that this had been an inside job by somebody with access to the warehouse. Police launched the largest investigation in the history of Quebec, dispatching over three hundred officers to conduct interviews with dozens of potential witnesses across all parts of the syrup supply chain. Finally, in December of 2012, eighteen suspects were arrested in connection to the crime. Eventually, twenty-six would be charged, including the suspected mastermind of the heist, Richard Vallières, a syrup producer with a grudge against FPAQ.

Vallières' father, Raymond, was also arrested for his involvement in the crime. Avik Caron, who owned the warehouse with his wife, was also charged for the theft. Caron had previously been convicted of multiple fraud charges. Police arrested Etienne St. Pierre, a New Brunswick–based syrup reseller who had acted as the fence for the heist, and Sebastien Jutras, the truck driver who had helped transport the barrels to and from the sugar shack where the syrup was stolen.

THE CASE TODAY

After a lengthy trial, Richard Vallières was sentenced in 2018 to eight years in prison, with an additional six-year sentence if he is unable to pay over $9 million Canadian in restitution for the syrup that was unable to be recovered. Caron was sentenced to five years in prison and fined $1,200,000 Canadian. Raymond Vallières and Etienne St. Pierre were both sentenced to two years of house arrest. The case remains the largest theft in Quebec history.

THE ITALIAN WINE AND CHEESE HEIST

Hard cheese and soft targets.

2015–2016 ★ *ITALY*

DESCRIPTION

Italy's Modena region is known the world over for its extremely high-end balsamic vinegar, wine, and Parmigiano-Reggiano cheeses. As Champagne is to the Champagne region of France, true Parmigiano-Reggiano is a regionally-protected product that can only be made in Reggio Emilia, the specific area of Italy that is home to Parma, Bologna, and Modena. As with fine wines, a good Parmesan cheese can only be perfected over time. Once the cheese has been properly aged, a 40 kilogram wheel can be sold for nearly $600 (€495).

Producing even a single wheel of the cheese requires between one and two full years of aging to create the characteristic flavors and texture. Reggio Emilia's landscapes are dotted with hundreds of enormous warehouses, each containing thousands of wheels of cheese or barrels of aging wine. Most warehouses sit on dairy farms or isolated country roads and are occasionally checked by cheese makers and vintners, but are usually left alone until it is time to add or remove the cheese and wine.

Between 2015 and 2016, teams of thieves descended on some of these warehouses and took full advantage of the lack of security. Late at night, groups of up to a dozen thieves would drive up to the warehouses in vans and trucks, slide open the doors and use flashlights to quickly identify which cheese would be mature enough to sell, before emptying the shelves and loading up their vans. Due to the large number of thieves on each heist, the teams were able to steal dozens of wheels of cheese in a matter of minutes. Once the haul was complete, the thieves prepared the goods for resale. Cheese makers marked the rinds of the cheese wheels with unique manufacturer codes and dates that could be used to track the aging, but these thieves quickly discovered that by breaking the wheels into smaller pieces, the cheese could still be sold quickly throughout Europe.

Other crews loaded trucks with thousands of freshly filled bottles of wine, sometimes stealing entire barrels that could be bottled and resold. Police estimate that the thieves had managed to steal at least 16,000 bottles of wine and more than 20,000 cheese wheels worth over $7 million (€5.75 million).

KNOWN SUSPECTS

In early 2017, authorities and farmers worked together to set up a sting operation called "Operation Wine and Cheese." What the sting lacked in branding creativity it made up for in efficacy. On March 20, 2017, police crept into a warehouse they thought might be the next target and settled into hiding places. Shortly after getting into position, a van carrying ten men— eight Italians and two Serbs—arrived at the warehouse. The passengers filed out of the van, but before they could make their escape, police made their move and arrested all of them.

THE CASE TODAY

Modena is still home to several vintners and cheese makers, who have pooled their resources together to improve the security of their warehouses and hire guards to conduct more patrols. While the number of thefts are significantly lower than they had been in 2017, there is always the looming threat that another ring of cheese thieves will come looking to make some cheddar.

THE HONG KONG TOILET PAPER HEIST

Even if it's recovered, you might not want it back.

FEBRUARY 10, 2020 ★ *HONG KONG*

DESCRIPTION

In the early days of the COVID-19 lockdowns around the world, panic-buying by consumers getting ready for quarantine led to bare shelves in stores all over the world, particularly in the United States and Asia. Scarcity led to astronomically high prices on the black market for everyday items, from canned food and bottled water to hand sanitizer. Perhaps no item was as sought after, though, as toilet paper, as uncertainty about the lockdowns created such a spike in demand that even Amazon sold out for weeks at a time.

During the peak of the panic buying, three thieves in Hong Kong's Mongkok district learned that a major grocery chain was expecting a restock delivery. On the day the shipment was due, the thieves waited near the store's loading area for the delivery truck to arrive. When the driver parked the truck and began moving to unload the supplies, the three thieves jumped into action. They surrounded the driver, brandishing knives and ordering him to open the back of the truck.

Once the door was open, they found themselves staring at a veritable treasure trove of toilet paper, and quickly stole over fifty packs or six hundred rolls with a retail value of approximately $220 before making their escape.

THE CASE TODAY

The thieves, whose names have not been revealed due to Hong Kong's privacy laws, were quickly found by police. Nearly all of the stolen toilet paper was recovered before it could be sold on the black market. During the trial, all three men pleaded guilty and were sentenced to forty months in prison, due to the premeditated nature of the crime. The judge also ordered them to pay back the value of the stolen toilet paper and apologize to the truck driver that they had robbed.

THE ELI LILLY PHARMACEUTICAL HEIST

America's largest pharmaceutical heist.

MARCH 13, 2010 ★ *ENFIELD, CONNECTICUT*

DESCRIPTION

Just after 9:30 p.m. on the night of Saturday, March 13, 2010, a tractor trailer backed up to the loading dock of the Eli Lilly warehouse in Enfield, Connecticut. The truck's driver and passenger exited the vehicle and went to the front door of the office. After verifying that there was nobody inside, the men went back around to the truck, where they grabbed a ladder and climbed to the roof of the nondescript beige warehouse. Once on the roof, the thieves found a thin spot and began cutting a hole through the tar-covered metal sheeting.

Once the hole was big enough for them to climb through, they set up a rope and climbing equipment and rappelled down into the warehouse. They went quickly to the facility's alarm and communication panels and exposed the wires. This alarm was fairly sophisticated; if the thieves cut the wrong wires, they would trigger a

silent alarm that notified police. One of them, an electronics and alarm specialist, had to disconnect specific wires to deactivate the alarm without setting it off. When the alarms were deactivated, they went to work disabling the surveillance system. Finally, they were ready to work.

They opened the loading bay door of the warehouse and backed the tractor trailer up close enough to sit flush with the ramp. Then, both thieves started up forklifts and loaded the trailer with pallets of pharmaceutical drugs, including Zyprexa, Prozac, and Gemzar. After a few hours of loading, they'd managed to fill the trailer with nearly fifty pallets. They closed the loading bay, and drove off with nearly $80 million in stolen drugs. Police were notified of the crime on Monday morning and began a thorough investigation. It was clear that the thieves were professionals, but they had been in too much of a hurry while leaving, and left behind several empty water bottles and most of their tools. These included a variety of hand tools and power tools, such as grinders and drills. They appeared to be new and were all made by Husky. Authorities sent the water bottles off for DNA testing but knew it might take time to get results back. In the meantime, they started looking into the tools.

Detectives learned that Husky tools are a store exclusive brand to Home Depot. Authorities were able to browse Home Depot's sales databases and searched to see how many purchases had been made with the exact combination of eight tools they'd found at the warehouse. Astonishingly, the search yielded only one result. The tools had been purchased in Flushing, New York, the day before the heist. Luckier still, the store had security camera footage of the purchase, and of the thieves loading the tools into the back of an Infiniti QX56.

KNOWN SUSPECTS

When DNA test results came back, police discovered that they matched DNA found in two similar warehouse heists in Illinois, and another at a GlaxoSmithKline facility in Virginia. The DNA belonged to a man named Amed Villa, though authorities did not yet have a name for the serial burglar. Villa and his brother, Amaury, both had extensive arrest records for burglary and lived in Miami, where they reportedly worked with another known interstate theft specialist known to authorities only as "El Gato."

A few days after the heist, authorities received an anonymous call stating that at least three people involved in the burglary would be meeting at a bar in Florida to discuss distribution and payment for the stolen medications. Police and FBI teams set up in the bar and watched as El Gato and two other men met to discuss the heist. Police initiated surveillance and quickly discovered that the heists were not the work of a few thieves, but rather a large, well-organized criminal syndicate that had its own fleet of trucks, sales teams, and teams that created and applied falsified labels to sell the drugs on the secondary wholesale market. The syndicate had stolen hundreds of millions of dollars in prescription drugs, tobacco, and other goods in multiple states.

When another anonymous tip pointed authorities to a storage facility, police used a set of keys left in a rental car used by one of the syndicate members to open multiple storage units within the facility. Inside the units were large amounts of stolen pharmaceuticals and supplies to repackage them for resale.

The FBI set up a phony wholesale pharmaceutical company and used a criminal informant to arrange a sale. Shortly after the sale, on May 3, 2012, local and federal law enforcement began making coordinated arrests of twenty-two individuals across four states. Among those arrested were Amed and Amaury Villa, and a man named Yosmany Nunez Aguilar who would be revealed as El Gato. Also arrested was Alexander Marquez, who had driven the tractor trailer from Connecticut to Florida immediately after the heist.

THE CASE TODAY

Amed Villa pleaded guilty to his role in the Eli Lilly heist, as well as several other burglaries in Virginia, Florida, Kentucky, and Illinois. On December 5, 2016, he was sentenced to seven years in prison and five years of supervised release. Amaury Villa was sentenced to ninety-eight months in prison and is required to pay $60 million for restitution. Aguilar received a seventy-month prison sentence and was ordered to pay back over $60 million in restitution.

THE UNDERWATER BEER HEIST

Not the kind of cold case you want when it comes to beer.

JANUARY 2021 ★ *ARGENTINA*

DESCRIPTION

Craft breweries are constantly seeking to develop new techniques and going to new lengths to create innovative flavors for their beers. A trio of Argentinian breweries tried to go to new depths instead, by aging their newest beer in a sunken ship on the ocean floor. On November 22, 2020, with the help of a local diving school, the brewers loaded 185 gallons of beer into seven barrels and tied them to the inside of an abandoned ship called the *Kronomether* more than sixty feet below the surface. The brewers had planned on allowing the beer to age in the ship for at least two months before retrieving it and combining it with another beer to create a 2,000 bottle batch of a hybrid brew.

Together with the diving instructors, the brewery owners took multiple trips to check on the beer, diving down into the boat to ensure that the intense pressure of the ocean depths had not compromised any of the barrels, and checking that the lines keeping the barrels against the inside of the hull were still holding. After a final check on January 19 showed everything looking normal, plans were made to come back on February 23 to bring them back to the surface.

Unfortunately, when the brewers arrived back at the *Kronomether* site to retrieve the barrels, they found only an empty ship and the severed ropes that had been holding the barrels in place. At some point during the last month, a team of thieves dove to the bottom of the sea, cut the barrels loose one at a time, and carefully swam them back to the surface. Then, the thieves presumably loaded them into their boat and drove off.

KNOWN SUSPECTS

Currently, there are no formally identified suspects, but police do know that because of the depth at which the beer was stored, scuba gear needed to be used. The *Kronomether* wreck is a fairly popular dive site, so it's likely that the thieves were nothing more than opportunistic divers who saw the kegs in the boat and decided to take them home, but police have not yet been able to rule out the idea of sabotage by another brewery. If sabotage was indeed the motive, it's possible that the responsible party just cut the barrels free and let the currents take them away.

Whoever took the beer, it's unlikely that they will be able to enjoy it, as the beer inside the barrels was not a finished brew, but instead an unpleasant and undrinkable concoction.

THE CASE TODAY

As of this writing, there have been no arrests or substantial leads in the case. The breweries and dive school do have plans to attempt another ocean floor aged brew in the near future, but are currently searching for another, less popular location to store their beer for the next batch.

ACKNOWLEDGMENTS

This book has been a labor of love from the beginning, in that I could not have done this without the labor and love of so many people. While I can't possibly thank you all, please know that it has been appreciated. Christina, thank you for your undying support and patience during this and every other endeavor. Thank you for your understanding during the many late nights and weekends I spent writing, and for being my partner in crime in everything we do. I love you, and I owe you many, many date nights. To my parents, thank you for supporting me and pushing me in all of my crazy interests while I was growing up, and for sparking my love of learning from an early age. Ryan and Tony, thank you for being my best friends even when I didn't know it growing up. I couldn't ask for better brothers, only better-looking ones. Matt, Coleen, John, Karina, Matthew, Joey, and all of my New York family: thank you for welcoming me into the family and making me feel at home from day one. John Sullivan, you've been the best manager I could ask for. Thanks for taking a chance on me, and for working so hard to get me so many dream projects, and for encouraging me to keep my own voice in each of them. To all of my friends in comedy and brothers and sisters in arms, thank you for the constant inspiration and nonstop laughs. Some of my fondest memories are the laughs we shared while running things by each other at all hours of the day. Originally, I was going to write these thank yous separately, but it turns out the army and comedy are pretty similar. To John Whalen and Margaret McGuire Novak, thank you for giving me this incredible opportunity and for working so hard with me to make it better than I could have imagined. Steve Cooley and Bryce de Flamand, thank you for your incredible design work and for making this book into a reality. Special thanks to Rebecca Pry for the absolutely jaw-dropping illustrations; somehow, you saw exactly what was in my head and made it better than I could have imagined. Thank you. Finally, to all of my podcast listeners, I couldn't have done this without you guys. Literally. Without you listening to *I Can Steal That!* and sending in topic ideas and growing the show, this book wouldn't be here. Thank you all.

ABOUT THE AUTHOR

Pete Stegemeyer is an award-winning comedian, writer, and physical-security and cybersecurity expert. Before becoming a comedian and writer, Pete served in the United States Army and deployed twice to Afghanistan. He is also the host of the popular true crime podcast, *I Can Steal That!* When Pete isn't working on research for his creative projects, he enjoys traveling the world with his wife, Christina, or walking around New York City with his two pugs.

INDEX

Names of heists are bolded.

E

Eiffel Tower, selling of, 68–70
Eli Lilly Pharmaceutical Heist, The, 208–10
empty chest (tool used in heist), 197–98
Enfield, Connecticut (city in which heist occurred), 208–10
Enschede, Netherlands (city in which heist occurred), 174–76
Escobar, Pablo (disguise as), 24–25
Europe (area in which heist occurred), 128–30
excavator (tool used in heist), 139

F

face mask (disguise used in heist), 134
First American Train Heist, The, 50–51
First Swedish Speedboat Heist, The, 16–18
Florence, Italy (city in which heist occurred), 194–96
Flying Squad, The (team in Scotland Yard), 138–40
Fortaleza, Brazil (city in which heist occurred), 81–83

G

gold, theft of, 10–15, 34–37, 50–51, 78–80
Golden Boos, The, 197–98
government bonds, theft of, 58–59, 78–80
grain sack (to hold stolen money), 58–59
Great Canadian Maple Syrup Heist, The, 201–3
Great Gold Train Robbery of 1855, The, 10–15
Great Pearl Heist, The, 128–30
Great Train Robbery, The, 46–49
Green Vault Heist, The, 162–64
grenade launcher (weapon used in heist), 78
Grizzard, Joseph, 129–30

H

hairpiece, theft of, 30–33
hairspray (tool used in heist), 151
hammer (weapon used in heist), 92, 146–48
hand grenade (weapon used in heist), 160
Harry Winston Paris Heists, The, 158–61

M

N

O

P

T

U

V

W

X

Y

Z

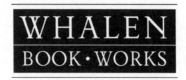

PUBLISHING PRACTICAL & CREATIVE NONFICTION

Whalen Book Works is a small, independent book publishing company based in Kennebunkport, Maine, that combines top-notch design, unique formats, and fresh content to create truly innovative giftbooks.

Our unconventional approach to bookmaking is a close-knit, creative, and collaborative process among authors, artists, designers, editors, and booksellers. We publish a small, carefully curated list each season, and we take the time to make each book exactly what it needs to be.

We believe in giving back. That's why we plant one tree for every ten books we sell. Your purchase supports a tree in the United States national parks. 🌲

Get in touch!

Visit us at Whalenbooks.com or write to us at
68 North Street, Kennebunkport, ME 04046.